# Confessions of
# an Ordinary Mystic

### By
### Jannel T. Glennie

FOREWORD BY RON DELBENE
ILLUSTRATED BY DON THOMAS

*for Virginia and Harold*

# Table of Contents

# Foreword

My friendship with Jannel Glennie began 20 years ago at a retreat center in Washington. At that time she was Director of Christian Education in a large church in Tucson, Arizona. She had come to the conference I was conducting in order to learn how to teach a simple way of prayer to those people in her congregation she knew were desiring a deeper walk with God.

As I learned more about Jannel during that week, I became aware of how down to earth she was–practical, caring and desiring to support people in their experience of God. I discovered that she had a gift for creating and designing exciting educational opportunities for people that led them to new insights about themselves and their relationship with God. I knew also that during that week Jannel was touched with her own spiritual insights and feelings, her own desire for a deeper walk with God.

Throughout the years of our friendship, it has been a privilege to see the many aspects of change and growth–including sorrows, decisions, discoveries and joys–that have taken place in her life. From time to time, Jannel invited me to be a part of her life in special ways. She welcomed me to lead programs and retreats for various groups. She asked me to preach at her ordination service. And now I am honored to be writing this foreword to her first book.

When I was reading her *Confessions of an Ordinary Mystic*, I remembered the many times she and I had shared about prayer in her life, whether it was around the meal table in the Glennie's dining room in Tucson, in the prayer room of a hermitage in the woods of Alabama, in phone conversations, or in Michigan at the church where she was ordained. No matter where it was, I always knew two things: Jannel was an ordinary person and Jannel was a mystic.

She has now arrived at a point in her life where she chooses to share some of her prayer experiences with us. In doing so she encourages you and me to recognize our prayer experiences and consider sharing them as well. She has a gift for not only telling us what she experiences, but also showing us how she reflects on and celebrates those events. She provides words and images to help us explain and explore our own spiritual insights and feelings.

I encourage you to read and rejoice in her story. I also encourage you to be attentive to your own story. My hope is that as you read her *Confessions*, her stories will resonate within you as they have within me–bringing renewed awareness of God's graciousness. Jannel reminded me again that each of us is called to be aware that we are ordinary mystics.

Ron DelBene

# Coming to
# Common Ground

# A First Offering

## (Or, Being Surprised by God)

> (W)e can experience God in this very life 'by many secret touchings of sweet spiritual insights and feelings, measured out to us as our simplicity may bear it.'"
>
> Julian of Norwich, 14th century English mystic

The first time I remember encountering God in an *other* sort of way was in 1980. I was sitting at my office desk, looking out at the south-western courtyard which formed the center of the one-story buildings surrounding it. I liked this office away from the other offices, and I liked this courtyard. It was simple — no showy plantings — only a grey stone bench, some well-tended grass and a large tree. Unlike the palms that were so plentiful elsewhere on the grounds, this was an old hardwood that survived the southwest heat.

This was my safe prayer space. I had just begun to practice a different way of praying. Meditation, I learned, was a way to listen for God – this was new to me. In the past, I had done all the talking, quite sure of what needed to be accomplished by God in my life, with my family and friends, and in the world. This new practice involved sitting quietly and repeating, over and over, a few words as a way to focus on God and on my heart's deepest need in hopes that they might come closer together.

On this day, I sat quite still, closed my eyes and began to pray the small prayer I had come to discover was my own heart's desire.[1] Its style was that of ancient saints who seemed very remote in time and place, certainly much holier and closer to God than I could ever hope to be. Yet this prayer seemed to seek me out as much as I sought it. It was so simple and immediately familiar. I played with the words – finding new meaning each time I reordered them. **Lord**, let me feel your love. Lord, **let** me feel your love. Lord, let **me** feel your love. Lord, let me **feel** your love. Lord, let me feel **your** love. Lord, let me feel your **love**. Such a plea it was! Somehow, I knew that if this prayer were answered my life would not be the same.

As I repeated the prayer over and over, I became aware of a shift taking place. It was as if I had become part of my own home movie. I found myself sitting on a bench, not unlike the one in the courtyard just outside my window, but this was clearly not the same place. In this new garden, I was seated on the bench, still saying my prayer. I knew I was not asleep since I could see myself sitting there. I felt I *was* there. I was also not disconnected from my office surroundings. At the same time, I was sitting on a bench in some garden to which I had never before gone. My eyes were open there. I could feel the stone beneath me. I continued to pray for God's love.

Much to my surprise a parade of children passed in front of me. Children of all nationalities, all ages, all sizes. They were all healthy, playful and happy. I spoke to them, played with them. Then they passed on out of my sight.

I became tired and left the bench to lie on the ground. It was grassy – such an inviting place I could not resist moving to it as it seemed to beckon me. I lay down on my back, looking up through the lacy branches of the tree above me. I felt contentment, total ease. Then I felt the earth move lightly beneath me. My whole body seemed to be dropping gently down into the earth. A body-sized hole with me in it was sinking down below the grass level. I was attached to the sod and moving deeper into the earth with it. I do not recall feeling frightened -- perhaps, a little unnerved and curious about this unexpected trick of nature; but I felt no desire to sit up or move.

A part of my consciousness told me that I *should* feel fear. What if the ground closed in over me like a tomb? What if I were lost forever? The experience felt so *real*. But a larger part of me remained content, intrigued, even "embraced" by Earth itself. Somehow I knew that all I needed to do was to exert a small amount of energy and I could *think* myself above ground again. After what seemed like a rather long time, my self-conscious fear got the upper hand. I remember saying, "I am not ready to be lost like this yet." Like an elevator lift the motion was reversed and I found myself once again lying on the cushiony grass of the garden, gazing through the tree branches into the blue sky. I returned to the stone bench a little dazed.

Within a few seconds I became aware once again of sitting at my desk -- really puzzled about what had just happened! The clock indicated that just five minutes had passed, though it felt like several hours. Is this what meditation was going to be like? What in the world did all that mean? What was I supposed to do with this experience, these feelings and images? I left the office and wandered outside, walking around in an effort to sort some of it out and regain my bearings. It made no sense to me, yet it was a clear, vivid memory. It remains so today.

For years I told no one about this puzzling experience. How could I tell it without the listener thinking I had lost my grip on reality? It was also so difficult to describe. No words seemed adequate, and still they do not. Since that first time, as I continue to pray my short breath prayer (though it

*I became tired and lay on the ground… on my back, looking up through… the tree above me… Then I felt the earth move lightly beneath me… I was sinking… deeper into the earth… embraced by Earth itself.*

has changed a few times in the past twenty years), I continue to be visited by visual, sensual encounters with Mystery. I have learned to value them, to journal them and to seek counsel in understanding them. I became committed to discovering more about such experiences, though at the time I was ignorant of any other companions along this way. This commitment has led me to read the accounts of the image-filled prayer lives of ancient spiritual leaders and to learn of their new understandings of God and of themselves as a result of them.

As I teach, preach and minister to people of all ages and in many different situations, I have come to realize that other people today, not just the ancient holy ones, experience intimate encounters with Mystery as well. They, too, are afraid of being doubted or accused of being out of touch with reality. They are confused and even frightened by the experience, not knowing how to sort it out or to whom they might go for help in understanding it.

The purpose of this book is to recognize and to affirm that people with all personality traits, faith backgrounds, levels of maturity, degrees of spiritual experience, religious affiliations or even commitment to regular prayer or meditation, have intimate experiences with God and God's creation. There are times when God breaks into our human consciousness in a way that is surprising and moving, even for a brief moment, and which is difficult to describe and often difficult to understand. Generally these experiences are not recognized or affirmed in religious communities except in a historical or theoretical way. Or they may be actively sought, made very public, and worshiped for their own sake. How many times have we heard someone who hears voices or *sees* things called eccentric, at best, or downright *crazy*. It took me many years before I could acknowledge my "encounters" first as valid and then as *mystical*.

Perhaps some of the difficulty lies in the confusion about what *mystical* experiences really are. First of all, most people refuse to acknowledge that they are possible or a *real* experience. If we do come to believe that we may hear or see things out of the ordinary, we worry about what others will think of us. As a result, few people who have experienced God intimately feel free to share their experiences for fear of ridicule, or at least uncomprehending stares, which might trivialize the encounter. Often we give little credibility to the event, thinking it is a silly dream and we dismiss it as inconsequential. Another fear may be that if we admit to such experiences people may expect more from us than we can give. As a result, people who have intimate, unitive experiences with the Sacred, rarely have the opportunity to appreciate or explore them fully. It is also true, I think, that we fear opening ourselves in the first place out of fear that we might invite undesirable, or destructive forces in. It is unfortunate when we miss the gift and meaning that true encounters with God can give to our lives.

This book is an effort to be explicit about mystical experiences and their implications for an ordinary person. I offer my confessions and reflections in an attempt to give value and encouragement to others. The format of this book provides opportunities for you to enter into images of prayer as vehicles for your own deepening experience of God. My goal is to show some of the ways that mystical experiences impact our lives and give us new understandings of God, of our relationships with others, and of ourselves. I include suggestions and guidance for developing an attitude that accepts the possibility of a new, expanded understanding of our relationship with God. If I accomplish nothing else, I wish to honor the ineffable, awe-filled nature of mystical experiences and suggest that these moments with God are not limited to ancient Hebrews, first century apostles or medieval saints. They have survived the rationalists in the Age of Reason and the materialistic, reality-oriented skeptics of the 20th Century. Mystical experiences endure because The Holy One perseveres in seeking us and desires that we become as fully ourselves as we were created to be.

This book is also for those who do not believe they have ever had an experience they would call mystical, but are curious about what it might be like. It is for those who may be able to name a moment when time and self-consciousness were suspended, being replaced with a new awareness -- but have never been able to tell anyone or discern meaning from it. It is for those who hunger for an intimate sense of God in their lives, but are not sure how it might happen. It is for those who have already established a deep, internal sense of God through intimate experience, and are looking for affirmation or companionship along the way. This book is not all things for all people, but I hope it will provide a window between ordinary living and the spiritual life, which can be extraordinary. I sincerely believe mystical experiences are not meant exclusively for saints and cloistered religious. I believe God is available and yearning for all of us who are willing to be open and receptive. The fact is that many of us have had these experiences already, but have not been able to identify them as such. They have slipped in through an openness which defies logical preparation. Such is the nature of Mystery!

# Common Ground
## (Or, What is a Mystic?)

The mystics find the basis of their method not in logic, but in life: in the existence of a discoverable "real", a spark of true being within the seeker which can (in an act of union) fuse itself with the object sought – God… [2]

Evelyn Underhill, 20th century English Mystic

One of the biggest barriers to my writing this book was naming myself a *mystic*. It seemed, and still seems, presumptuous to adopt such a lofty identity for myself. At least the definitions I had read and the people I knew to be true mystics all indicated that to be a mystic one had to be better, higher, wiser, holier, certainly closer to God, and definitely more disciplined in her prayer life than any *ordinary* person. I always thought a mystic either lived in seclusion or in a community outside the mainstream of *normal* life. Do mystics really clean the toilet, nag their spouses about home repairs, pump their own gas (or even own a car!), read frivolous novels or eat too many chocolate chip cookies? Don't *mystics* pray constantly, enjoy hours and hours of centered, undistracted silence, and disdain the worries of normal everyday living? None of the latter apply to me. Yet (and it is a big YET), I have experienced God directly and intimately many times; and I have heard stories from others who can also immediately identify such moments for themselves. Another big YET is that the very act of writing this book has been an up-and-down, on-and-off, roller coaster ride encounter with God. Nevertheless, I am quite ordinary. But first come the confessions!

Most of us associate the word *confession* with an admission of a wrong-doing. We confess our sins. We acknowledge in that confession our guilt for things we have done or have not done which have caused pain for others and ourselves. Mostly, we think of confessions as uncomfortable times at their best and excruciating at their worst. They are times when we make public, or semi-public, our failings and our vulnerability. But this is not the sense at all in which I offer this personal material.

Confession is also an expression of awe. Confession is acknowledging that we are part of a much greater whole than what we normally notice. It is a recognition that there is more going on in the world than the eyes, ears, nose, tongue or fingers can sense. It is appreciating the sacred presence that breaks into our consciousness quite surprisingly. It is a deep knowledge that God is seeking us as much as we are seeking God; and, there are times when we become especially aware of this dynamic process.

These moments of encounter with the Holy may include new insights or wisdom, healing, self-understanding or direction. They may just be the pure, simple feeling of being loved. They may drive us to our knees or set us flying. They may stop us in our tracks or give us the courage to move forward. We may recognize them at once, or it may take years to realize we had a God-moment. Sometimes they are "mountain-top" experiences. Often it is simply a growing awareness of subtle changes in our lives made possible because of God's prompting.

To acknowledge these moments may not, however, be any easier than the admission of sin. These are holy moments which are difficult to describe, hard to recognize and harder still to trust to someone else. But, just as confessing one's sins can make, or begin to make, things right in one's life, confessing moments of awe and union with God can foster spiritual growth and self-understanding. I have benefitted by the confessions of others brave enough or foolish enough, or simply *compelled* to go public.

I offer my experiences and reflections here as a way to affirm other ordinary people who have experienced the sacred mystery in the midst of ordinary living, but have been reluctant to acknowledge them as mystical or even real encounters. I offer them also for those who yearn to know God more deeply for themselves. Perhaps my experiences will provide a springboard for your own new awareness of God's convergence with your life.

First, we must come to some common understanding of what I mean by *mystic*. When I explore a new topic I usually start out with many more questions than I do answers. Generally, I end with at least more informed questions! What is it about mystical experiences and mysticism that captures our attention and interest? In the last decade the number of books and articles on people who have reported encounters with the *other* is amazing. We love stories about angels, people who have survived death to report their *other side* experiences, and miraculous appearances or manifestations in the most unexpected places. We have easy access now to texts written by mystics of the middle ages which were previously considered unworthy for any scholarly or theological consideration. These are currently widely read and valued.  It is not unusual now to hear chant written by one of these mystics being played on a popular radio station. Clearly, we are searching for something that is beyond ourselves, which can give new meaning to our lives. Or maybe it is just curiosity. Whatever your reason for picking up this book, I suspect you, too, will come away with more questions. This is good for it may lead to your own discoveries.

What is a mystical experience and what is it not? To begin with, a mystical experience is a unique, memorable moment which is like no other. Perhaps it can be likened to a gem, a marvelously cut, multi-faceted gem which we have just discovered. We are about to hold it up to examine the clarity, the cut, the angles, the shape, how light is reflected within and outside of itself. Of course, we can only see certain facets and never all of them at once. We can never fully define or describe it. It may change because of the way we are holding it or because of the amount of light or our ability to see. The more we know about it the more we can appreciate its beauty, even when we discover imperfections. Unlike a gem, however, the mystical experience is a living, loving, moving, apprehending moment. Still, we must learn all we can – though we can only explore a limited number of perspectives.

The words *mysticism, mystics, mystical experiences* may conjure up for you a number of different assumptions and implications. For some people, mysticism is simply a type of confused irrational thinking not linked at all to the way we are expected to think every day at work or even while relaxing. Others may associate it with *spiritualism* (worship and communication with the "spirit world") and *clairvoyance* ( the ability to "see" into a realm beyond this tangible world), or even *occultism* and *magic*. "It may also be associated with obscure psychological states and happenings, some of which are the result of morbid pathological conditions. Still others may use it as a synonym for otherworldliness or to describe a nebulous outlook upon the world, or a religious observance."[3]

Christian mysticism is most often relegated to the contemplative saints, dedicated religious types, who lived more than a thousand years ago. They are the ones who gave up their ordinary lives for prayer and contemplation exclusively, and then reported some out-of-the-ordinary experiences. Mostly, we call them extra-ordinary, certainly beyond anything we would expect. At some points in history these people were seen as wise ones to be sought out for guidance. At other times they were run out of town, excommunicated from the church, thrown into prison or burned at the stake. Francis or Clare of Assisi, Hildegard of Bingen, Dame Julian of Norwich, Teresa of Avila, John of the Cross, Evelyn Underhill, Meister Eckart, many more saints and many, and many little known, unnamed or unrecognized folks form a solid foundation for a *real* mystical spirituality – ordinary human beings experiencing God in a unitive, intimate way.

We shouldn't wonder at the confusion around mysticism. The word *mysticism* comes from the Greek *muo*, to close. This verb described, in particular, the closing of the eyes. The terminology of mysticism was first used in connection with the *mystery religions*.[4] The term then was used in association with a secret or closed experience. What one could experience, another would have a difficult time understanding. This then described the very unique, personal encounter between a person and God. At many times in history those who had not had such an experience were very skeptical about others who had. In some cases, this was not just a benign opinion, but instead resulted in persecutions. Is this so very different from many experiences that we try to recount to someone who wasn't present? How can they really appreciate the shared emotions, the circumstantial humor, the *electric* group response, or the memories that were triggered by the event?

Mysticism is not limited to one religion, nor is it limited to organized religion at all. Mystical writings have been found in all cultures. Many of the images or themes recur across time and geography by men, women, children and groups. Mystical experiences are not limited to ordained religious leaders or theological scholars (in fact, they may be least likely!). Mystical spirituality is certainly not limited to Christianity. All religions to some degree or another recognize those who, through their traditional doctrine, are led to the Holy One in an intimate way. For some the very heart of their faith is seeking such a union. Some societies hold behavior that we westerners label *mentally ill* as honored and mystical. While mystical experiences are not ordinary everyday occurrences, I do believe ordinary people may have mystical experiences.

Mystical experiences, as I understand them, and will use the term, relate to a time when a person gains consciousness of a wider reality, a sixth sensing. It is a closeness to God or a feeling of deep intimacy with The Holy which we cannot *think* into being. This experience may involve images, or it may be a feeling, an understanding, a knowing, a revelation which clearly comes from a source outside or deep within our self. You may ask, "How *could* I have thought of such a thing?" Behind all forms of mysticism there is the belief that an intimate and direct relationship with God or with *transcendent reality* is possible. Most importantly, such experiences result in some outward change. In Christian Scripture, Jesus taught, "Those who abide in me and I in them bear much fruit." (John 15:5b, NRSV). We cannot encounter God and expect to be left unchanged!

The image of a mystic as someone with his head in the clouds, totally out of touch with reality is very limiting and just not true. Even Teresa of Avila, 16th century Spanish mystic, and her nuns had to perform the menial, hard work of daily survival, and administer the mundane details of convent living as well as saying prayers. The mystic must be grounded in the real stuff of living, for that is where we are most human, most real and most open. Evelyn Underhill, a 20th century English writer and observer of the spiritual life, saw communion with God as practical and very attainable.

> Where the philosopher guesses and argues, the mystic lives and looks, and speaks, consequently, the disconcerting language of first hand experience, not the neat dialectic of the schools… [W]hile the absolute of the metaphysics remains a diagram — impersonal and unattainable — the Absolute of the mystics is lovable, attainable, alive.[5]

Perhaps because of her "practical" spirituality, Evelyn Underhill wrote one of the most definitive books on mystical experience, *Mysticism*. Her practical essays on the spiritual life in relation to one's everyday existence became a popular radio program in England. They later were collected and published. While she never claimed to be a mystic, nor wrote of any extraordinary experience, she clearly knew of which she spoke and wrote. Her life was witness enough to her deep faith and wisdom.

Historically, those who have tried to be alone, to live the life of solitude are the ones we label *mystics*. Yet it appears that their isolation in prayer did not discourage people from seeking them out. Even those who chose the cloistered life, were sought out by townspeople, royalty and popes for advice. They were seen as wise ones whose dedication to God enabled them to see life more clearly. Some were able to share their insights and wisdom within the religious community. Others chose to live apart in a cell attached to a church or even a mountainside cave, being called *anchorites*. The reality in all cases, is that these mystics were rooted in reality, grounded to the society in which they lived, even if they chose to withdraw from the busyness of the world. In a very real sense they created a window into the church and a window into the world, while remaining reflectively enclosed. They were princes and paupers, wealthy women of society and last daughters who sought escape from ill-conceived marriages. They came to their unique life in their youth or in their later years. Many were brilliant, talented men and women. Some were able to write about their experiences; others died with their experiences cradled in their hearts. Some sought the lifestyle of prayer, others were led to it most unwillingly at first.

Arsenius was a well-educated Roman of senatorial rank who lived at the court of Emperor Theodosius as tutor to the princes. While still living in the palace, Abba Arsenius prayed to God in these words, "Lord, lead me in the way of salvation." And a voice came saying to him, 'Arsenius, flee from the world and you will be saved.' Having sailed secretly from Rome to Alexandria and having withdrawn to the solitary life (in the desert of Egypt) Arsenius prayed again: 'Lord, lead me in the way of salvation' and again he heard a voice saying, 'Arsenius, flee, be silent, pray always, for these are the sources of sinlessness.' The words, *flee, be silent and pray* summarize the spirituality of the 4th century desert fathers.[6] These words still sum up the life of a mystic – even a "sometime" mystic – and even if *fleeing* only means escaping to one's bedroom.

Some folks would psychologize themselves around, about and away from mystical experiences, saying that they are just a voice or message from one's sub-conscious. It is hard to find a therapist who appreciates insights gained from religious or spiritual sources, let alone from God! (I must admit I was in a quandary as to how to answer the question on my psychological exam for entrance into seminary as to whether or not I had "heard voices.") I think I worried about the question of how mystical experiences are related to psychology more in the beginning than I do now. I studied psychology in college. I read Jung and Freud. I came to appreciate the difference between behavioral and depth psychology, a systems approach and other methods of understanding the human psyche. Some of my favorite people are psychologists! I have come to see that the study of our psyche is not all that far from deep experiences of God which reveal truths about ourselves.

The way I see it, psychology is the recent human construct for trying to understand who we are and why we do what we do. Spirituality, of which mystical experiences are a piece, is an ancient cooperative effort with God to become closer to our original creation — which was proclaimed Good! Both seek to help people become healthier, more whole individuals for themselves and in their relationships. I see them very connected, indeed, and not mutually exclusive at all.

For instance, many psychologists consider dreams important ways to access hidden feelings and truths for an individual. So do I. I would even go so far as to say that I believe that God participates in – provides? – dreams for the purpose of helping us discover ourselves more fully and to promote healing. But there is a difference between dreams and mystical experiences. Dreams act themselves out while we sleep. We may observe ourselves dreaming, but we really don't cooperatively participate in them, except to draw ourselves out of a bad dream and awaken. Mystical experiences are waking experiences, and while we cannot create them, we may become our own actors, voicing concerns, expressing emotions, conversing with another "character," and participating when the opportunity arises. God desires our cooperation, promotes our freedom, gives us choices. It is our own fears, limitations, narrow mindedness, woundedness, cynicism or bull-headedness that keeps us from resolving those very things in our personalities. A therapist can help in some ways. It may take a prayerful experience with God to help in others.

Following are descriptions of some encounters I have had with the Holy over the last twenty years. Mostly, I am an image person and *see* these encounters. Therefore, it is my hope that the illustrations as well as the words may help you to envision the event. More importantly, I hope that they can be windows through which you may see the Sacred more clearly for yourself. You may discover as you look at the drawings or read about the encounters that something similar has happened to you. Or you may be reminded of something you have not thought about in years. I hope you will use the white space on the page to write or draw your insights and responses.

I have also included some brief reflections that come from my attempts to gain meaning for my own life through these experiences. The reflections are not exhaustive interpretations or detailed explications, since the encounters hold many levels of meaning and continue to present new insights for me even after twenty years. The reflections do offer ideas about universal themes that occurred to me in the encounter and which may be relevant for anyone. I have also included some ideas and questions in the Appendix which may guide you into deeper reflection – alone or shared in a group.

After several encounters I offer some suggestions and guidance about becoming more open to God through disciplined, intentional practices. They are not a formula that guarantees mystical experiences! They are guidelines for engaging us – body, heart and mind – in the act of faithfulness. These practices – or disciplines – confirm our love for God, our desire to be in relationship with God and our commitment to do our part. They offer some practical things we can do to be attentive to God in our lives and, therefore, to open the door for God's presence and our growth.

The last encounter is a way to say Amen! to all of God's gifts. It acknowledges the mundane and the mysterious, the small and the large ways our lives are touched by God. These blessings are gifts for us but they also send ripples out into the world affecting people we might never meet. Anytime we come to know the love of God intimately it is a blessing for which we must give thanks.

This book is not meant to be a definitive book on prayer, meditation or spiritual disciplines. It is not meant to be the last word in mystical experiences. In sharing some of these God-encounters with others in the past, I discovered that many people said my sharing had helped them on their spiritual journeys. I hope they will encourage you to discover your own images, your own relationship and encounters with God. I hope you will find some tools which might be helpful for you to understand yourself better, to deepen your relationship with God, and to find your place in the world.

*Encounters, Reflections*
*and, Guidance*

# Introduction

And I have felt
A presence that disturbs me with the joy
of elevated thoughts; a sense sublime
Of something far more deeply interfused,
Whose dwelling is the light of setting suns,
And the round ocean and the living air,
And the blue sky, and in the mind of man,
A motion and a spirit that impels
All thinking things, all objects of all thought,
And rolls through all things.[7]

Wordsworth, *Tintern Abbey*

Following are excerpts from my journals which attempt to describe what I had just experienced. In nearly all of these cases, I had gone apart to a quiet place. It may have been a few days at a retreat center or hermitage, or it may have been in my bedroom. I generally begin by creating a space around me and an open space within me. Sometimes, I light a candle to give myself a focus and to remind me of God's presense. Sometimes, I just sit comfortably and close my eyes. In all instances I begin with a *breath prayer,* a short repetitive prayer of seeking. After a few moments the prayer becomes a mere pulse in the background like an electric current, connecting me to the source — acknowledged but unseen. Or it may be like our breathing — it is happening, but I am so accustomed to it, it goes on without any attention on my part supplying the oxygen I need to live.

I am always surprised when an image emerges behind my eyelids. I am not asleep. I may even be aware of a bird outside the window, the furnace banging, an airplane roaring overhead, or the tiny ticking of the overhead fan. Still, my inner attention is drawn to the image offered me. As if on cue, the cameras begin to roll, a scene appears, and I become part of the unfolding drama. In the midst of it, I may laugh, cry or experience physical sensations. I may even have conversations with whoever is presented to me. Because my faith is rooted in the Christian church, the images that appear are likely to come from this tradition; however, I have been surprised by some rather non-traditional figures who are clearly from God and not my experience of church. One indication for me of such a gift is that I could never have created the images or the message through my own willpower.

I do my best just to allow the experience to take place, not forcing a situation or outcome but just letting it emerge. I have also learned to trust that I can sort it out later when I journal or talk with my spiritual director. Trying to examine it or analyze the experience while living it may destroy it. It really is best to let it emerge as it will. As long as I maintain my breath prayer, recognizing God as always present, I have no fear of any other spiritual intrusions.

Some of the experiences that I offer are complete, some are snippets of much longer ones. All are difficult to describe because of the limitations of language. Some meditations lasted five minutes, but felt like days; others may have taken an hour but seem much shorter. As an alternative way to appreciate the encounters, there are also illustrations which interpret the experience. You may want to just look at the pictures before you read the encounter – too see what you might see before reading my description. There is plenty of white space for you to make notes or comments.

Each experience is followed by a brief reflection or meditation on some theme that it suggested or, perhaps, a learning that I gained from it. I make no attempt to fully explicate each experience. Some insights came to me immediately. Some have only become clear after many years and much reflection. This is the nature of a relationship with God. Levels of understanding continue to be revealed the deeper we dive into the encounter. In the beginning, our search for understanding seems very complex, but the more we work on it the more there appears to be some order or pattern to it. If we persevere toward understanding, in fact, the answer lies in simplicity. The more we encounter God, the more we discover truths about ourselves which, in turn, reveal the wonder and connection to the world around us.

Images and conversations are not the only ways that we discover God's intimate presence with us. Sometimes, the simple acts of faithful persistence create the opportunity for us to see ourselves more clearly and to experience God more deeply. These experiences may be just as mystical as *seeing* the face of God. Therefore, I also offer some spiritual practices which draw us deeper into the spiritual life. These are tools which you may use to continue to see the presence of God for yourself. As in any relationship, there are things we can do to enhance and deepen the connection to reach a greater intimacy and knowledge of each other. If a marriage is to be all that it can be, the couple must be committed to intentional work on communication skills as well as offering each other physical expressions of love.

Friendships require honest, reciprocal sharing of time and life stories. So it is in our relationship with God. If our goal is to seek God's presence more fully in our lives, then there are some things we can do to encourage the relationship and foster the opportunities for better communication and deeper love.

Following each set of encounters and reflections are some suggestions for ways that might help deepen and enhance our relationship with God. Spiritual disciplines provide a map which helps us travel the many pathways between God, ourselves and our world. They provide guideposts and boundaries, detours and signs. They draw us forward and give us space to rest. They draw us inward yet help us live in the world more responsively and responsibly in union with God.

Let us now risk this adventure together!

# Black God

As I sit in my room preparing to pray, I begin by softly singing the new breath prayer (*Set me free, Lord, set me free*) -- funny, it reminds me of the background music a choir might sing for a black preacher. The next thing I know there is a black preacher standing before my inner eyes on a raised platform and I am the choir and the congregation -- by myself. There is music in the background. I am sitting out in the first pew. Somehow, I know the black preacher is God. He is about 6' tall, a little stocky, dressed in a black suit, lots of laugh wrinkles on his face. He talks as he walks back and forth across the stage. I am fascinated by his hands. They are large, expressive hands always in motion, often directed toward me. He is engaging, compelling, powerful -- especially because of his deep, melodious voice. He is preaching to me.

He says, "Honey, you are free, but let's talk about it some. "Love -- yes, I loved you from the beginning. Remember how much your father loved you? That was my love too. Everyone loved you as a child. That is why it is so easy for you to love me now, so easy for you to love your family. Love is no problem for you, though do not forget to show it.

And then there is trust -- Oh, yes! there has been some struggle with that. That's where you got confused about pleasing people and mistrusting yourself. Remember if you love yourself, you are loving me — AND if you trust yourself, you trust me. Trust…

(*To be continued…*)

*I know the black preacher is God... He talks as he walks... I am fascinated by his hands. He is preaching to me!*

# Black God Reflections

## Images of God

"Behind all forms of mysticism there is the belief that an intimate and direct relationship with God or with *transcendent reality* is possible, and that this constitutes a mode of existence and a mode of knowing which is different from and perhaps superior to normal existence and knowledge. There is usually a sense of the union of the person with a wider reality. They often speak of union with God…"[8]

Kenneth Leach

The definition most frequently given to mystical experience is *union* with God or the sense of Other. While in such a union, we do not lose a sense of self, we gain a deeper *knowing* about God -- and, in turn, a deeper understanding of ourselves. Also, in the process, we might be surprised at how we see God.

This encounter with The Black God came to me when I was on a retreat in New Jersey in 1984. This retreat was designed to be eight days of total silence, with short presentations offered by a retreat director. It was my first retreat of this kind, and I was a little nervous. I had taken time away for prayer and reflection in the past, but not is such a large dose. I brought with me a discipline of praying a short repetitive prayer during times of silent meditation and any other time of the day I could recall it. As far as I know, the prayer request itself was the trigger for this unexpected uncounter, as nothing else had been suggested by readings or the retreat director. My Breath Prayer continued to be *Set me free, Lord, set me free.*

Both in God's teaching and in God's image I am met by my prayer request. What better way to be instructed in freedom than through the preaching of a black God?

How do you imagine God? What kind of a relationship do you have with this image of God? What would you ask God? You might try to be surprised by a new image for God. What new truth does it offer?

# The Corral

## (Encounter with the Black God, continued)

Then there is freedom, Honey. You have been getting free all along. Imagine yourself as a colt in a corral. The corral is there to protect the colt as it gets its legs. It lopes freely, but within the fence. That is what I've been doing with you, Child. At first, the corral was pretty small, but lately it has gotten bigger and bigger. Those times of waiting you were talking about earlier are times of new and bigger corrals. You just need time to know the space within the fence and also to know your boundaries. Right now you have a pretty big field in which to run and play and discover… you need lots of space to grow – but there will always be fences for you to tend to and to protect you.

[I feel him leaving and I call to him to stay, but he says it has been enough. I returned to this preacher several more times in the week as he had important lessons to teach me. I did not see him again after this week.]

*Imagine yourself as a colt in a corral. The corral is there to protect… know the space within the fence… know your boundaries… There will always be fences.*

# The Corral Reflections

## Freedom

Freedom does not mean doing anything you want to do. It means really wanting to do what you must do to open up all the taut teguments of the flesh to the power of the Spirit.[9]

William McNamara

*Teguments,* I discovered, is a layer of material or skin that covers or encloses -- both restricting and protecting. What a good way to describe this corral and the discipline of *freedom*. Freedom is one of the essential elements of faith from which we draw wisdom to make decisions; to respond to others; to pray, to play and to love. Freedom is an essential step in the spiritual journey of becoming a whole, healthy person. Freedom allows, it does not enforce. It invites without closing off. It is the gift given humanity by God from the beginning.

Freedom requires discipline and boundaries like the fence of the corral which may be expanded, but which support and give definition. We want our toddlers to become strong walkers, but we do not let them walk in the street to practice walking. Too often we decide not to teach our children one particular religion in order to allow them to be free to choose for themselves. Yet they then have no outline of faith upon which to base their choice.

Guidelines, boundaries and disciplines provide a way for us to grow into a trusting relationship with God and ourselves. Our perception of the gate may depend, however, on our experience with being *contained*,[10] having someone else make decisions for us about our freedom. The spiritual disciplines may at last allow the imposed restrictions to fall away, and then we notice that the gate was open all along.

What does freedom mean to you? How does freedom relate to your spiritual life? How free do you feel? What experiences have you had of being *contained*? Which disciplines or guidelines have given you the most freedom? Do your actions coincide with your internal sense of freedom?

# The Forest

I found myself walking into semi-darkness – a mist was all around and the ground was rocky. I knew I was to climb the hill that was a short distance away and right in front of me. I was afraid, but somehow knew I would not turn back. Then I realized there was someone else near me holding my hand and arm so I would not fall. I didn't expect the help, but I wasn't surprised either. Curiously, I could see myself – but a few years younger.

I began to climb the hill with the help of the unidentified friend. Then the ground began to change and it became like shale or malachite. It was very dark – reminded me of the cave where the Golum (from J. R. R. Tolkien's *Hobbit*) lived. I didn't think I could climb on that slippery rock with no path and no obvious footholds; but, my friend kept holding my arm. We climbed into the blackness.

Finally, we reached the top but there was another hill. This one had a road, and looked easier to climb. It was rocky and rutted in places, even muddy. On one side there were yellow marigolds lining the way. The other side had a few blue cornflowers, a couple daisies but mostly greenery – myrtle and spent peony bushes. At first, the road was quite wide and I wandered back and forth from one side to the other. My friend was still there but I didn't need him to hold my arm any more – just to walk near me.

The road began to narrow. The marigolds were fewer and fewer, then gone. When I stood at the narrowest end of the road, I thought I saw a dense deep forest with only a narrower path. I thought I would have to go through that forest and I despaired. I had reached my limits. I just wouldn't walk in the darkness on rough paths any more, and I said, "No!"

*I found myself walking in a forest in semi-darkness… and the ground was rocky. I was afraid, but somehow knew I would not turn back.*

# The Forest Reflections

## Guidance

If you should at times fall, don't become discouraged
    and stop striving to advance.
For even from this fall, God will draw out good.
Even though we may not find someone to teach us,
    God will guide everything for our benefit,
provided that we do not give up.
There is no other remedy for this evil of giving up prayer
    than to begin again.

Teresa of Avila, 16th Century mystic

How many of us would venture out on a long journey across country without a companion. And if we did strike out on such a trip alone we would still take maps, consult a travel agent, change the oil in the car, or call ahead for reservations. We would have to pack and have some idea how we would finance the trip. Today many of us would also have our cell phones handy.

Setting out on the spiritual journey, or more importantly, staying on the journey requires some of the same preparations, precautions and care. Too many people think they must travel this journey alone. That may mean that they never even start out. Or it may mean that they find themselves wandering in a wilderness unsure where to go next -- no map, no guide -- just an urgency to go. They may not even be very clear about where they have been.

Those who are serious about pursuing their spiritual journey need help along the way. This help may come in a variety of ways. A wise man or woman may give us an insight that helps us turn the next corner. A book may reveal a path that we had not considered. A supportive community may provide respite when we can go no further. A question asked, a sermon preached, a story told all may provide the impetus to keep going. We may even choose one person to serve as guide, director or fellow journeyer.

Who has provided guidance for your journey? When did you find yourself lost or unsure where to go next? Where do you find your best support? What else might you do to stay on your spiritual journey? When did you say "No! It is just too hard!"? What helped you continue? or not?

*Finally, we reached the top, but there was another hill.*

# The Path Reflections
## Finding a New Way

Two roads diverged in a yellow wood,
And sorry I could not travel both
And be one traveler, long I stood
And looked down one as far as I could
To where it bent in the undergrowth.

Robert Frost[11]

As much as we would like to flee from the moments of pain and darkness in our lives toward the light when we believe all will be right, it is my experience that there is an important time between acknowledgment and real lifestyle change. It might be described in a number of ways. Perhaps it feels like the arduous walk uphill which we did not anticipate, but we realize is the only way out. This is a journey which may require that we go slowly, finding a new way, working hard to stay on a new path. The dark places are often places of solitude and transformation. Living into the new life which we have been given may require more energy and close attention than we imagined. It means adjusting our expectations of God and of ourselves. It may mean significant lifestyle changes. Occasionally, we are so ready to be out of the dark and prepared to see a new way that we race gleefully into the light.

We might also be tempted to turn back into the wood, the dark place. The road looks long and the destination unknown. So we ask: Where am I being led, anyway? How can I know it will be better than where I have been? At least we are familiar with our past experiences. Perhaps we even think it will be different, better when we go back this time. But it never is. Our hope is misplaced. It can only be by the new road that we will find the life-giving way instead of the life-defeating way. The change must come from within us.

When have you experienced a time in your life when you were looking down a new road? What obstacles stood in your way or choices did you see in direction? What other image might you have for the time after darkness? What companionship do you seek along the journey? What do you imagine could be over the hill?

# Being in Place

## Prayer
### (Or, Discovering a Relationship with God)

If we ask of the saints how they achieved spiritual effectiveness, they are only able to reply that, in so far as they did it themselves they did it by love and prayer. A love that is very humble and homely; a prayer that is full of adoration and of confidence. Love and prayer on their lips are not mere nice words; they are the names of tremendous powers, able to transform in a literal sense human personality and make it more and more that which it is meant to be…

Kenneth Leach[12]

When I was a little girl living in rural Michigan, I can remember spending an amazing amount of time alone – given the fact that I had four brothers and a sister. Perhaps, my mother was too busy to notice that I was gone, but I spent most of that time outdoors. I have vivid pictures of my sitting under a huge oak tree making acorn tea cups and saucers. Then I would serve my guests and we would have a lovely party. I recall climbing down the hill near the creek and the bog filled with yellow cowslips. I would sit by the little pool that captured the spring-fed water before it overflowed into the creek. Mostly, I made crowns, necklaces and bracelets out of snake grass pretending to be queen of the world – beloved by all and loving all. Then my brothers would find me and we would hike through marsh and woods to the park that was once training grounds for soldiers. We would play war among the fabricated ruins.

One recollection that has come to me many times over the years is my walking down the country road between our house and my Grandmother's just up the hill. I walked along that route many times, occasionally picking up beechnuts, but mostly just whistling. Sometimes I would sing – loudly – my arms outstretched in dramatic passion. As I would whistle or sing, I imagined that a Hollywood talent scout would drive by in his yellow convertible and stop when he heard my whistling. He would lean out of his car, a look of wonder on his face, and ask me my name. Then he would tell me what a wonderful whistler I was and did I want to go to Hollywood and be a star. I suspect I would have responded with something like – I'll have to go ask my mother.

These times of being alone and imagining, I believe, were the beginning of my prayer life. As I look back at the image of the little girl and the talent scout from this perspective I can imagine anew that it might have been God seeking out my talent and my innocent wonder and love. This is the purest prayer there is: God seeking us and our responding in innocent wonder and love. The relationship begins. Prayer is initiated.

Prayer, for me, tends to be very broad in definition. How many books are there on prayer? I have read and tried many different forms. There was a time when I did more *trying* and less praying. Since that time, I have resisted trying to limit certain actions only as prayer. Even to distinguish word prayers from silent prayers is unrealistic since most of us think in words anyway; so the words may not have been spoken, but they are there nonetheless. The bottom line is that prayer is *being in relationship with God*, with the Holy One. Prayer is our efforts to come to know better the One who is beyond us and within us, the One who created us and generously offers us pure unconditional love in spite of everything we do to resist it. Prayer is seeking the One who is already seeking us – turning ourselves around to face and greet Mystery.

If prayer then is our efforts at relationship, then the name we call God is a reflection of our understanding of that relationship. While God is Power beyond any human being we know, we still search for familiar words to bring God closer to us through our experiences. After all, it was God who told the first human beings to name the contents of the world. And so our beginning efforts of relationship are contained in the very name we use for God. Father. Mother. Holy Wisdom. Jesus. Lord. The Inner Light, the

Deepest Abyss. Creator. Mother Earth. *Adonai.* Spirit of Life. Abba (Daddy). The variety of names for God are too many to list here. Then there are all the adjectives that describe the work of God and the way God has appeared throughout history. God is omniscient, omnipresent, omnipotent. God is loving like a mother hen, generous as a benevolent monarch, or stern as a righteous judge. God travels in a pillar of smoke, creates hardship to teach a lesson and provides food to sustain the faithful. God heals, calls, gathers, disperses and works miracles. The names and descriptors we use for God are the beginnings of prayer, for they create images which seem to make God more accessible. Once God is accessible, we think, perhaps we can relate to God.

In the beginning, before we were *enlightened* by rational thought and scientific reasoning, it was not so much work to pray. The ancient ones saw that the creation of the world and all that was within it was well beyond their capabilities, and so they were glad to acknowledge that only God could have accomplished such a feat. They saw the earth, animals and themselves as all part of a whole which already was in relationship, including God. Clearly there were phenomena which occurred in spite of human action – to these, they gave God full credit. Even the most advanced cultures recognized and appreciated the Power in nature and in their lives. Relationship with the Power was essential to live and to live well. The Israelites, in Hebrew scripture, were clearly reliant on God and sought God's blessings on land, flocks and family. Prayer was life and life was expressed in prayer. God's mystical ways were accepted without question. While there was a great chasm between God of the universe and human beings, God was still the loving, omnipotent parent. The human response was to respect and love God in return. There were also times, in the process of developing the relationship, that angry words were exchanged, destruction and rebellion were rampant, testing and fleeing were more common than loving companionship. Both God and the people of God struggled with just how the relationship would take shape, but, after God hung the rainbow in the clouds after the Flood, the covenant took hold and God agreed never to break the relationship again.

According to Christian scripture, the connection began to break down on the human side. So God sent Jesus, to teach a new lesson and to reestablish the loving relationship. When God became human, women and men learned new ways to relate to each other and to God. God became more accessible, yet still mysterious. Jesus Christ became the link between God and humanity. The stories of Jesus living among the faithful and the unfaithful, the clean and the unclean, the wealthy and the poor, gave a context for God which both assisted prayer and complicated prayer. At the very heart of it, people came to such renewed love and commitment that they were willing to die for that love.

As time passed after Jesus' death and resurrection, the stories of his life and work were recorded and spread throughout the world to change the character of human relationship with God forever. Through Jesus, people believed they could have a much more intimate relationship with the Holy. People came together to form communities where the early church remembered and ritualized the critical events of his life as ways of living out that faith. The sacraments became times of real God consciousness and God presence. The community of believers became a sacramental representation of Christ's presence in the world and to each person individually. Through the remembering and the ritual direct contact with God was expected. Prayer was essential to maintaining the relationship and being obedient to Jesus' teaching.

I will leave the telling of a complete history of how prayer has changed over the next 2000 years to others. It is important to note, however, a certain evolution that has brought us to where we are today. Attitudes toward prayer have come a long way from the assumption of God in one's life and the natural response of prayer to the uncertainty of God's presence and a feeling of inadequacy to pray. We have been influenced by the birth of many schools of theology that have taken the role of interpreting God and our relationship with God for us. As scholars and priests began to classify, analyze and compartmentalize the world, the spiritual life also came under scrutiny. Just being in relationship with God – calling upon God at any moment of the day, in verbal prayer or in silent awareness – was replaced with prescribed methods, appropriate words and designated experts.

Not only was prayer classified and categorized, but individual responses were observed, pigeonholed and judged. Knowing God intimately (mystical experience) was separated from wise thoughts about God or *right* worship. From those divisions then, it was concluded that only certain people could pray in those certain ways. Theologians *thought* and preached about God. Religious (monks and nuns) *experienced* God through their sacrifice and constant devotion. Clergy *said* prayers on behalf of the people.

Eventually, many assumed that only the very bright could really understand God and only the *ordained* could really have a relationship with God. Meditation and contemplation became the tools of expert pray-ers and ordinary people began to lose confidence in their own ability to relate to God directly. In fact, mystical experiences, ecstatic, intimate encounters with God were finally seen as dangerous. Scientific thought and the Age of

Reason further eroded belief in the ordinary person's ability to trust that they might experience God, or, for that matter, trust that there was a God in whom they could trust.

The twentieth century did nothing to improve the situation. With the clear divisions of denominations, faiths and spiritual practices in place, one group became suspicious of another and some classic, traditional prayer practices were abandoned because they became associated with another group. Meditation has been seen as an exclusively Eastern tradition. Spiritual realities like *being born again* or *speaking in tongues* tend to be relegated to a particular brand of Christianity. With lines drawn and sides taken, classical traditions of prayer have been lost or lumped in one camp or another.

Yet there continues to be a yearning toward God. And, in fact, people really never stopped praying. Many just went underground or re-formed the categorization to include groups that not only permitted, but encouraged – even required – the direct experience of God. Once we are aware of the challenges and false assumptions about prayer, we may find ourselves free to explore our relationship with God more critically. We may find that we have been caught in the rational, logical thinking that limits God for us. We may really believe that someone else will pray better than we can. We may have drawn the lines between religious groups so firmly that we cut ourselves off from time-honored methods and spiritual gifts that could greatly benefit us. The fact is true prayer is not so concerned about technique, only about seeking God. That is not to say that our intellects should be cast aside, for after all, they also are gifts from God. Rather, we might do better to trust the wisdom of the heart and to observe more carefully the assumptions we bring to the act of praying.

I use the word, *prayer*, to mean any effort we make to initiate relationship with The Holy One. Prayer is our good faith attempt to communicate with God. It is our acknowledgment that God is there -- waiting to hear from us. The other half of this communication equation is our listening for God's response. After all, any good communication requires these two parts: the talking and the listening. Since these are two different, but related actions, I am describing them as distinct disciplines. Prayer is our establishing the conversation; meditation is our listening. I will discuss the discipline of meditation in the next section.

Prayer, in the broadest sense then, is acknowledging and inviting God into anything that we do or say. It may be a mindful walk in the woods, recognizing the beauty, the extravagance and the complexity of creation. It may be the experience of music – singing, playing or listening – which draws us out of our normal consciousness into a new consciousness and which elicits emotional or even physical response to the presence of the Holy. Prayer is movement – dancing or running or digging in the soil. When our bodies are in motion we may tap into an even greater awareness of the full relationship we have with the Incarnate God. Prayer is loving a friend or caring for a stranger. It is recognizing the pain or anger in another person – or in ourselves – and calling upon God for help, realizing we do not have to bear it alone. Prayer is a kind word, a compliment, an apology, an expression of gratitude, an outburst of joy.

Prayer is shaking our fist at God, demanding why things are as they are or weeping for the injustice in the world or a desperate grief. Prayer is admitting our doubts but hanging into the relationship anyway. Prayer is admitting our failings, our thoughtless, mean-spirited acts, our prejudices and hate but holding onto God anyway. It is also our desire to make things right. Prayer is – or can be – our work, our play, our loving and our service to others. Just as I could not list all the names of God, I could not list all the ways that we might be in prayer and *be* prayer. The key to identifying an act as prayer is the awareness of God as involved, committed companion. The awareness might come in the midst of the act or it may come after the fact – as in my little walk to Grandma's house.

Unfortunately, prayer has been scared out of many of us. Lord knows that we would never want to be called upon in public – even among friends – and especially among relatives – to pray aloud. We might get the words wrong, or we fear our minds will just seize up and go blank. We think we are not doing it as well as someone else we know who *really* prays. Therefore, I suggest a style of prayer which can transform daily activities into prayer and ground whatever other forms of prayer you are currently using.

At the beginning of this book, I referred to a short repetitive prayer that was transformative for me, a style of prayer that I have used for over twenty years. It is a way one may pray constantly throughout all activities. This form is ancient and has been described in a variety of ways. The desert fathers of the fourth century, monks devoted to prayer, sought to maintain a constant awareness of God. They called it the prayer of the heart. For them, there was no need for lengthy prayers. Instead they insisted on simple words which would not get in the way of God. John Climacus wrote, "When you pray do not try to express yourself in fancy words, for often it is the simple, repetitious phrases of a little child that our Father finds most irresistible. Do not strive for verbosity lest your mind be distracted from devotion by a search for words."[13]

Within the cloistered life, men and women memorized the Psalms and repeated them as they went about their work. In the Eastern Christian tradition, a form of constant prayer took several different forms, but came to be known as the *Jesus Prayer*[14] in *The Way of the Pilgrim*. Its goal is to lead one from a prayer on the lips to a prayer of the heart. Most recently, Ron DelBene (priest, spiritual guide, and author), in his book, *The Breath of Life*, describes more fully the way one might discover her own *breath prayer*. It is a small prayer which calls upon God by name and expresses the pray-er's deepest need. This style of prayer is often known as a *mantra*, repeating one word or a few syllables over and over in silence, as a way to stay centered on God, to remain aware of the relationship and to grow in faith.

This style of repetitive prayer enables us to *pray unceasingly* which, in turn, keeps us true to our faith and true to our heart. The prayer can be used during times of quiet, or it can be repeated anywhere, anytime. Quite surprisingly, the pray-er learns that one can do several things at once, such as change a diaper and pray at the same time, or prepare for a sales presentation and pray, run a marathon and pray, wash the dishes, endure bumper-to-bumper traffic, and paint a picture – all the while praying. Ordinary tasks become ways to come to know God better and take on new perspective as well. We can discover God in the most surprising places.

This prayer form may establish deep roots into the spiritual life, from which other forms or expressions may flourish. It does not depend upon specific religious doctrine or theological teaching, though it is rooted in the Christian understanding that God's love and grace are generously accessible. Launching ourselves on such a discipline may also create a hunger to discover more about other forms of prayer or a community of faith. Such a discipline acknowledges that we desire God and God desires us. Taken into silence, the *Breath Prayer* seems to create space to listen, because it becomes as much a part of us as our breath.

Once we open the door for God through our intentional acts of prayer, we must be prepared for a new life. Isn't that what getting to know a new friend is about – or discovering new dimensions of an old friend? Talk with a couple who have been married for 50 years or more. They will tell you that they may know each other's habits, but they do not fully understand the other. And they will tell you that each has changed the other's life. *If it weren't for James, I would not be the person I am today. If I had not met Kristen, my life would never have taken the turns it did. If Becky were not my friend, I would not have pulled through my difficult times.* Friends and lovers change us. They offer possibilities we could never have seen for ourselves. They challenge our assumptions and encourage our weak wills. They hold us when we don't know which way to turn. They offer insight and clarity when all we can see is fog. They drag us out to play when we think we must work harder. They bandage our wounds and forgive the unforgivable. They call when we least expect it and send flowers when we think they forgot. If this can happen through *ordinary* people, how much more might we grow and change through a friendship – or loving relationship – with God?

Simply put, prayer is making the effort to establish, maintain and grow into a relationship with the Holy One. Prayer is acknowledging that God desires to meet us, to love us. It is our willingness to open ourselves to that love. Whatever we do to foster that relationship may be called prayer – words or no words, still or moving, in verse, prose or set to music. It is not so important to learn a *right* way as it is just to do it.

# Meditation
## (Or, Listening for God's Response)

One who has wife and children, crowds of servants, much property, and a prominent position in the world can yet attain the vision of God; it is possible to live a heavenly life here on earth… not just in caves or mountains or monastic cells, but in the midst of cities.

Symeon the New Theologian, 11th century monk[15]

Many people think that meditation is for the truly holy, saintly people who can devote themselves to hours of silence, uninterrupted by working for a living, caring for children, maintaining a house, or having any fun. Meditation, we think, is only for the serious pray-er who is able to sacrifice worldly commitments. Or we may see it as time wasted, non-productive, when there is so much to do. Even those who have given it a try often conclude that their minds are just too busy to sit in silence – since the silence isn't very silent. We are much more comfortable filling our time with "real" experiences – *necessary* experiences. We move from one engagement to another, sometimes frantically. We rely on our day planners or Palm Pilots just to keep track of where we are to be next and what we are to do. Such is the condition of the successful life, which is clearly defined as the *busy* life. Just the thought of taking what we perceive as doing-nothing time makes many of us very nervous. But I wonder what our lives would be like if we did stop occasionally for a moment of quiet. What might we learn if we have time to reflect on our last encounter, before we get engaged in the next one? How might we come to know God better?

Meditation is the discipline of taking time to listen for God. Meditation is the other side of the prayer conversation. If prayer is, indeed, engaging the relationship with God, then there must be some time set aside to hear the other side of the conversation. When do we give God a chance to be known? If prayer is our efforts to seek God, then meditation is making space for God's response. It is quiet time. It is silent time. But it is not wasted time! Just as we must set aside time for being with the people we love in order to deepen our trust and love of them, we must also allow such time for being with God if we desire a deeper experience of God.

We may decide to spend this time in a variety of ways. Making time for God is not unlike deciding how to make time for friends or loved ones.

Our approach can be a very well-planned, choreographed time set firmly into our schedules, or it might just be stopping alongside the road en route to the next appointment or between loads of laundry to breathe deeply, give thanks, or sit quietly with an open mind and heart. How we listen for God is as diverse as our personalties and our level of desire to know God's love more fully in our lives.

After I had attended Ron DelBene's conference/retreat on prayer and discovered how the *Breath Prayer* could be used in meditation, I was excited and determined. I thought I could manage only five minutes each day of attentive silence and reflection using my newfound breath prayer, *Lord, let me feel your love*, as a guide. After being in silence, the idea was to jot down a few sentences in a journal about what the experience was like. What words or images came to mind? What new feelings did I notice? I thought I could manage this much space in my busy day.

Once I returned home, however, the actual task of setting aside five minutes every day was much more daunting. Where could I do it without interruption? When could I find time in my already crowded days? I didn't want this to be another flash-in-the-pan prayer "high." I thought through the logistics of such a discipline. The place? My bedroom. The time? After work when the children would be occupied with their books and games. I knew meditation would be lost in the flurry of morning activities, and it would mean *sleep* if I left it for bedtime. I had a plan, but what is it about silence that invites interruption?

I got comfortable in my bedroom with the door closed and locked. The children were occupied. My husband was still at work. I began the simple ritual preparations of lighting a candle and reading a line of scripture. Just as I closed my eyes to focus inwardly on those few centering words, I heard a little scratching on the door. I tried to ignore it and gain the wonderful focus I had experienced on retreat. More scratching. Then a small voice, "Mama, maaaama, what are you doing in there?" My immediate reaction was anger and the urge to respond, "Can't you leave me alone for five minutes?" Perhaps the prayer mood had already been created within me, and through divine intervention (I am sure!), I refrained from that explosive response. I went to the door, invited my four-year old daughter into the room and asked her if she would like to join me in what I was doing. I told her to sit next to me and be very still. I explained that I did this very thing whenever I went in to the bedroom after work and closed the door.

I knew this would not be quality silence. Who could attain that illusive inner peace with a four-year old staring at you? But I persevered in the *attitude* of silence anyway; and, before long, she quietly slipped off the bed and out the door. The mystery of what mother was doing behind closed doors was solved. She was doing Nothing! Actually, her older sister was on to me! I could hear her answer the phone, and, in a rather disdainful voice announce that I could not come to the phone at the moment. "Mother is *meditating*!"

There is always something that will threaten silence. It is a void which wants to be filled by every distraction in the world. We are a world of words, sound bytes, fast moving images and pressures to be productive. Silence and inactivity go against the grain of our lives. A few moments of silence in the elevator feels like an eternity. At the other extreme, there are some for whom silence is a constant companion and represents loneliness and isolation. In either case, attentive silence can be daunting, like standing in front of a door which promises to reveal calamitous mysteries. We may feel like Indiana Jones, with all the trials – trap doors, snake pits, fraying rope bridges and utter darkness – before us if we open it. Worse yet, we may fear we will not have any experience at all.

Actually, our time in silence may reveal some unexpected things. I certainly was not expecting anything like the encounters I describe in this book when I opened my door to silence! I did not necessarily think of silence as frightening or threatening, only unfamiliar. I must also admit that I wondered just what good it would do; but after my first experiences of silence, I knew I really *wanted* and needed this time in my life. I was married, raising two young children, working, going to college full time and trying to become a committed member of a Christian community. If the result was nothing more than having five minutes to myself, I decided that would be enough.

Instead of life-threatening encounters, I discovered life-giving images. I discovered that silence was one important time where I could be totally myself and feel loved, challenged and supported – all those things I mentioned under prayer that good friends do for you. *Being in place* is the invitation to discover God in spite of and in the midst of our daily distractions and to remain centered. Being mindful of making little spaces between the things that we do allows God time to intervene and may make our lives more focused and peaceful as well. Making time to listen gives an opportunity to hear our own hearts beat and even as we discover God we discover ourselves more fully. We cannot manufacture mystical experiences, but we can place ourselves in the position of being ready for God's life-giving friendship by creating a space of open expectancy, a readiness to listen, and a willingness to respond. That is what I believe meditation is: open expectancy, pausing in the Presence, expecting that something will happen, trusting God's friendship. It is listening for God's response to our innermost needs and feeling Love in return.

Bookstores and, now, the internet are filled with books written on the *right* way to meditate. Many of these are very good. The most important thing is to choose one style or method that fits for you and to stick with it. Find a way to put yourself in a place of expectant listening. Keep your expectations reasonable — more is not necessarily better, though there may come a time when the silence begs you to stay longer, to come back again soon. Remember that learning to meditate — developing a new style of prayer — is like learning anything. We feel awkward and preoccupied with the method before relaxing into a familiar routine. Again, this is very much like any relationship which needs constant attention for it to grow. The discipline of setting quiet time aside is worth the effort, for not only do we come to know Mystery more intimately, we also come to know ourselves better within it and because of it. Where we have not found words before, we discover them. Where we have relied on them too much, they fall away, to reveal a new image of ourselves.

# Solitude
## (Or, Pausing in the Presence)

You already know that God is everywhere… Do you not think it matters little for a soul with a wandering mind to understand this truth and see that there is no need to go to heaven in order to speak with one's Eternal Father or find delight in Him? Nor is there any need to shout… He is near enough to hear us. All one needs to do is go into solitude and look at Him within oneself, and not turn away from so good a Guest…

Teresa of Avila[16]

Community may be much easier to comprehend than existing alone. In fact, we are wary of anyone who wants to be alone for any length of time, let alone for a lifetime. We think that all single persons ought to be dating, living with someone or, of course, married. We distrust the idea that they are truly happy. Few parents raise their children to value time alone (unless it is punishment!). We try to get them involved in groups, on teams, always directed and busy with one thing or another. But, just as Jesus of Nazareth sought solitude in the mountains or in the garden to balance the times spent with the multitudes, we too must find the balance between company and being alone.

Solitude might take some getting used to. Once extended silence begins to seep into our consciousness, however, she is an alluring companion. Five minutes of meditation may not be enough time after you have become accustomed to the practice of quiet. In the normal course of work and living you may notice that small silences that used to disturb and agitate you become more comfortable and the words of others are intrusions. Gradually, we may be led into longer times of prayer or meditation, but even that does not seem enough. When this happens -- or when you just can't seem to find any silence anywhere -- it may be time to consider a time away for extended solitude or retreat. This is a time dedicated to leisurely, attentive silence.

Retreats can take many forms. I find that the word *retreat* is used rather loosely these days. Any time that is taken away from home, whether it is for business planning, continuing education, or recreation is called a *retreat*. While this is not bad, it can be misleading when you attend what should more correctly be called a conference expecting to find a retreat, in the classical sense of the word. A retreat is a time which is designated primarily for silence and reflection. There may be a retreat director providing prayer exercises, reflections, meditations and individual consultation (direction), but there will also be significant time set aside for individual quiet. It may also be time taken by an individual alone in a hermitage, retreat house or private cottage. Sometimes, a retreat can even be accomplished without leaving home.

After several years of making annual retreats of four to six days, I realized one year that I did not have the money or time to leave home, nor could my family afford for me to be gone. In desperation, I called my spiritual directors and asked if it might be possible to make my retreat right where I was -- at home. They were intrigued by the possibility, and we discussed how we might do it. After some discussion, we decided that I would be given some relevant reading based on my concerns and needs, and I would set aside time while the family was away at work and school to "be on retreat." I still had to pick children up from sports practices and prepare something to eat, but that was it. The rest of my duties could wait. I would call my director each evening at 9:00 to review the day and process any questions or insights I had.

With this plan in mind I read, prayed and kept a journal of my observations and insights. Of course, the washing machine broke down and I had to call for repair, and more salesmen came to the door than I could ever remember in one month, let alone one week. Through it all I was able to keep an *attitude* of silence if not *actual* silence, which began to permeate the house after the first day. My favorite chair became my retreat center. It was important time for me, and as it turned out it was good for my family. Our house felt "prayed in." I had many new insights and a renewed sense of direction, but I also realized how essential retreat time is wherever we take it. We must claim the solitude we need — if not just for ourselves, for the good of those with whom we live. Retreats benefit everyone.

It is a good habit to plan a few days away once a year. It may also be possible to take one day away every three or four months. If you have never had time away alone, you may wonder what does one do on retreat? Can you really spend all that time just praying? The best way to begin is to arrange time under the guidance of an experienced teacher who will help you shape your day and activities. She may help you design a pattern of your day or a focus that would suit you. You may also find a book that guides you through the days. Often, religious orders will offer directed retreats which provide a structured format of presentations on an aspect of the spiritual life, preaching, times of silence, and time for conversation with a director.

Recently, I arranged a couple of days away with our two daughters just before our older daughter's wedding day. All of us were in the midst of transitions — marriage, vocational decisions and changing family dynamics. We took this time away simply to be together. I came with no agenda, no ulterior motives, no instructions – though my daughters were a little suspicious at first. But they soon fell into the habit of saying less, reading when and what they wanted, sleeping as needed, walking in the woods, or just sitting on the deck entranced by the sunset. It was important time, life-giving, holy time.

In the solitude of retreat, we are able to make space not only for God but for ourselves as well, in times of contentment, crisis, transition or, in fact, anytime. I should add that not all retreats are peaceful. The holy space that we give ourselves might become a time of discovering long avoided pain, grief or anger. Retreats are not escapes – though they give us space away from daily pressures and demands. The *Wounded Heart* drawing came out of such a time. In an effort to accomplish daily expectations of us, we often tuck away, in some deep compartment of our soul, a painful memory or shameful act. It is the only way we can get along. Eventually, however, it must be addressed or the secret act begins to interfere with our healthy living. One way to help nudge it out into the light is through activity. Retreats do not just mean sitting in one position all day seeking the ever-elusive silence. Walking, drawing, playing an instrument, dancing, singing, writing, practicing an exercise such as yoga or Tai Chi – even massage (if you are fortunate enough to have the option) – can release the bonds that hold us captive to a secret. It seems that our muscles hold memories as well as our minds and hearts. Then through God's grace, we can begin the healing, reconciling process that is possible.

Times of solitude might bring into clarity a difficult decision that needs action which we have been avoiding. They may press us to face our own sin or self-destructive behaviors. We may become aware of being part of a larger system which degrades or destroys God's people and creation. The mystical way is a way of self-knowledge as well as God-knowledge. St. Teresa of Avila wrote to her community of nuns, instructing them in prayer, but not as a way to seek a profound experience of God about which they might boast. Rather, she taught them how to pray so that they would come to know themselves better and appreciate the deep love God had for them. Teresa wrote:

"The fears come from not understanding ourselves completely. They distort self-knowledge; and I'm not surprised if we never get free from ourselves, for this lack of freedom from ourselves, and even more, is what can be feared. So, I say, daughters, that we should set our eyes on Christ, our good, and on His saints. There we shall learn true humility, the intellect will be enhanced, as I have said, and self-knowledge will not make one base and cowardly."[17]

How can we ever come to know our inner wisdom, as well as our fears and insecurities, if we do not spend quality time with ourselves? Gaining self-knowledge is not always a painful, serious matter. In fact, I doubt that God wishes that to be so as much as we do. Times of being alone with God and ourselves may also entice us to dance, to create, to sing, to feel true joy and pride in who we are or what we have overcome. We may discover the peace that is so fleeting in our normal course of living and move us closer to an even deeper peace that underlies all living.

Solitude may lead us into union with The Holy in amazing ways and, in the process, gives us new clarity about ourselves and our relationships. The mystical way is not a path that moves us away from humanity but very much into the midst of the world. How we live out the experience of knowing God intimately in our own lives is up to us.

*Being in Place* is a way of living with an awareness of God always present to us. This requires attending to our relationship with God in a very intentional way at the most unusual times as well as the most expected. Prayer, meditation and solitude are disciplines we can incorporate into our lives to foster and enliven our awareness of God's love for us. They are also the tools we can use to come to know ourselves more fully and to become more and more the people we were created to be.

The hard part is that these disciplines require us to change our lifestyles to find time, in the midst of already full, busy lives, to carve out new spaces and to develop new habits. *Being in Place* may begin with a few prayers in the morning and then grow to five minutes of silence in a closed bedroom. Then our yearning extends to silent time away and gradually it emerges into an awareness that this silence may be felt at anytime and anywhere. It is then that we notice the real changes taking place. The most surprising things grab and hold our silent attention – sunsets, rain drops, faces of loved ones or strangers, dogs, trees, dilapidated tenements, glorious gardens, or burned-out forests.

*Being in Place* is a growing understanding of the effect our words have on others and our actions have in the community. *Being in Place* raises our consciousness of the motivations and influences that determine our patterns of behavior. We might also discover that we feel less lonely, whether we have people around us or not, and more fully alive. *Being in Place* is an attitude of gratitude for life and a willingness to be surprised out of our narrow viewpoints about ourselves and the world.

Prayer, meditation and solitude prepare our hearts for God's grace and love. Moments of silence hone our senses to appreciate God's transformation of mundane moments into sacred encounters. As a result, ordinary people become more than ordinary.

# The Garden

I placed myself once again in a prayerful position and recalled the images of the day before — the hills, rough roads, the darkness and the forest ahead of me. I could see myself standing on the road at the bottom of the last hill, but instead of the forest the scene before me had changed dramatically in twenty-four hours.

The forest had disappeared. In its place was a garden. It was a beautiful garden with many paths and fountains and benches and water gardens with lilies. The colors were wonderful and bright. The sun shone. It was a complete contrast to the scene of the day before. What a surprise!

At once, I knew this was no ordinary garden. I heard a voice saying, "How could you have missed my signs. Remember all the cards?" (I had been feeling very sorry for myself since the surgery and hospital stay.) I did remember all the cards I had received wishing me healing — prayers for me. They had been like shafts of light coming toward me from all directions. I wept in gratitude for those healing prayers — for all the people who remembered and prayed for me — and believed God would heal me when I had doubted. I was greatly humbled.

More tears, and my perceptions broadened to include those who have died who continue to pray for us — the cloud of witnesses. And in that moment, I realized that my mother (who had died 20 years before) also prayed for me and helped in the healing. I sought her presence; and, she came to me. We talked as if she were standing in the room with me. I told her it was time to let me go — for me to let her go. I asked her to let me be the woman I am now — to let me go. I think she had been waiting for me to ask. Without my really knowing how — I realized we both let go. I said, "Shall we dance?"

We were back (many years) on Grandpa's front walk at a family gathering with the polka music blaring. We danced like we never had before — with great abandon and joy.

Then something changed. I was still dancing, but I was no longer at Grandpa's house. I was no longer dancing with Mother. I was back in the Garden dancing down the cobblestone path. This time, I danced with the Stranger, whom I now know was Jesus. We danced all through the garden, never stepping on the flowers, but with great delight. The Spirit blew in the trees and the sun was warm on my back.

*We were back on Grandpa's front walk… the polka music blaring… We danced with great abandon and joy. Then something changed – I was back in the Garden dancing down the cobblestone path. I danced with Jesus.*

# The Garden Reflections
## Self-understanding

Mysticism entails a definite Psychological Experience. Mysticism shows itself not merely as an attitude of mind and heart, but as a form of organic life. It involves the organizing of the whole self, conscious and unconscious, under the spur of such a hunger: a remaking of the whole character."

Evelyn Underhill, 20th Century English Mystic

To think that what we experience or have experienced in all facets of our lives does not pertain to our spirituality or to our relationship with God is too limiting for our own good. We may try to compartmentalize our lives in an effort to control *what* we do *when* and *how*, but the fact is we are one WHOLE person and each part affects another. When we invite God into our consciousness, the primary task (if not *only* task!) becomes knitting us back together as we were *knit together in our mother's womb.* (Ps. 139, NRSV) Therefore, coming into relationship with God means coming into better relationship with ourselves, which is the process of healing. This convergence is especially felt in the mystical experience.

For the most part the medical model that pervades our culture is a mechanical metaphor. When a part goes haywire, we fix it or replace it. That is the cure. In healing, we must be concerned with all parts of the body when one goes *haywire* – body, mind, emotions, and spirit. In the Garden experience, a very deep part of me which I thought had been satisfied re-emerged after a surgery. Recovery provided a space for my Mother and Jesus to converge within me, letting go of one and embracing the other. I might have *thought* my way out of the last apron string to my mother, or *psychologized* my way through childhood memories, mother's death and my feelings of loss. Instead, I joined the Dance of the Spirit that goes much deeper than either one and moves down the path of healing.

When do you feel most compartmentalized? Most whole? When have you experienced a convergence of body and spirit, or mind and emotions, or all of them at once? In what areas of your life do you desire healing?

# Wounded Heart

*From time to time I have found it helpful to explore my relationship with God and what is in my heart through physical expression. I have used pastel crayons, large sheets of paper and music to help break through what seem to be barriers to my understanding. I often use my left hand to avoid directing and judging the work. What appears on the paper frequently redirects my vision to where I can find new access through the barrier.*

*At this particular time, my life was in upheaval with many changes, disappointments, new plans, new roles, increased expectations on me, comings and goings. I described myself as "a shell of a vessel through whom God flowed leaving nothing for me, but nourishing everyone else."*

When I began to draw, I chose the colors first – yellow, orange and red first – then purple – then black. The orange and yellow formed the top and bottom borders – a design leaping raggedly back and forth across the page. In the center was an intense orange half-circle – open at the top. I remember reaching for the red and pressing hard to make two circles next to each other of deep red – on top of the orange half circle. Next the purple seemed to leap out of the red and orange circles. Only the black was left. I could not ignore it though I knew it would radically change the picture. The black became a thick line across all the other colors and anchored in the red circles. The thick, jagged line stretched from one side of the page to the other. There was nothing more to add. The music and the colors had drawn me deep within myself and revealed a truth that had been hidden from me before. The energy I expended through my finger, hands, arm – my whole body – unlocked a knowing I cound not have learned in any other way. I fought the urge to flee to the surface again quickly and judge my work.

*… yellow, orange and red first – then purple – then black… the music draws me into the colors. The music and the colors had drawn me deep within myself.*

# Wounded Heart Reflections

## Pain

At such a time I pray to God:
'O God, this burden is too heavy for me!"
And God replies:
"I will take this burden first and clasp it close to Myself
and that way you may more easily bear it.'
But still I feel that I can bear no longer the wounds God has given me,
unanointed and unbound…
I am hunted, captured, and bound,
wounded so terribly that I can never be healed.
God has wounded me close unto death.
If God leaves me unanointed, I could never recover.
Even if all the hills flowed with healing oils,
and all the waters contained healing powers,
and all the flowers and all the trees dripped with healing ointments,
still, I could never recover.
God, I will tear the heart of my soul in two
and you must lie therein.
You must lay yourself in the wounds of my soul.[18]

Mechtild of Magdeburg, 13[TH] century German mystic

Union with God is not escape. In fact, mystical experiences are likely to offer us a look into our deepest pain. There is no hiding from God. It is inescapable. There are no masks or artful disguises, for the Holy One is Truth. Whether the pain is from abuse, neglect, sin, grief or depression, it cannot be hidden from God. Whether it is self-inflicted or imposed upon you by the world, it cannot be hidden from God. Whether we believe God has *given* us the pain or we understand it as human-made, God is part of it -- and part of the healing. To think that mystical experience is always ecstatically joyful is to miss the point of the relationship. To deny the presence of pain or loss results in setting up a barrier between us and God, and, inevitably, between us and those we love. However we do it, we must move through the barriers to become whole once more – to learn to love and trust again or more fully.

What are the colors that you would choose to *paint* your internal life? How would you describe or draw your areas of pain or discomfort? How has healing taken place in your life? Where might it yet take place? What colors would you use?

# Wounded Heart Further Reflections

## Sin

Several years after having this colorful experience, I saw something else. It occurred to me that *pain* is a by-product of *sin*. That is not to say that all pain is a result of our own sin. However, pain is often a result of someone's sin, if not our own. Sin never lives in isolation. It always wounds someone. *Sin interrupts living.*

Sin is . . .

> … seeking power above all else — even over people we love
> … being separated from God
> … not following the commandments
> … not listening to our heart's wisdom
> … breaking faith or covenant
> … missing the mark
> … fooling ourselves into thinking an unjust act was justified.

There is no getting around it. We all do it. The difference may be whether we can acknowledge it and seek forgiveness – whether we are willing to take responsibility for it and express remorse. The consequences of unresolved sin are hardness of heart, a reluctance to sin less which create life-denying patterns, loss of freedom for we shackle ourselves!… and pain, for ourselves and others.

What sin is interrupting your living? Yours? Another person's? What could you do to soften the heart? Seek forgiveness? Make recompense? How is your freedom restricted because of *missing the mark*?

# Falling Leaf

[I was fascinated by a leaf that fell as I watched out the window of my retreat, and wondered: How does a leaf know when to let go?]

spring green, fresh, cool
        clinging with all my might
            to the branch,
            feel the freshness
               the breezes
                  the wind
                      the rain tingling;
            a bird rustles past – in a hurry –
I cling still, tightly.
warm sun,
        warm rain pushes, moves, threatens
            but, I cling to my greenness
            and to my branch
            for it feeds me
cool darkness
        stirrings of change within me
            and around me
               I am not hungry.
        my greenness fades… only to surprise me
            with red
It is still loss
        I am losing my grip
            No more food.
sun still glows, but cooler yet
        I know my time is short
        I sense separation
            wholly changed now
               no more pain,
                  red fades to brown
I must let go
        there is no choice –
                  surprisingly pleasant
                    feeling the breeze… touching
              rustling,
                hurrying,
                      falling,
                pause,
                No – hurry on…
                     to rest.
How peaceful to finally let go.

# Falling Leaf Reflections

### Making space and letting go

To look at any thing
If you would know that thing,
You must look at it long:
To look at this green and say
"I have seen spring in these woods;
          will not do -- you must
Be the thing you see
You must be the dark snakes of
Stems and ferny plumes of leaves,
You must enter in
To the small silences between
The leaves,
You must take your time,
And touch the very peace
They issue from.[19]

John Moffitt, 20th century American poet

    I like to think I can control my destiny as much as anyone, yet I fight to find a little space in my life to let it all go. This kind of thinking sounds way too confused! How can we want both control and, at the same time, want time with no control? I suppose the very act of carving out time to *not do anything* is control -- or is it? Is this a spiritual issue? Yes, I think it is.

    The ramifications of how we decide to use our time – how we use others – affects our relationships, our job satisfaction, our attitudes about play and recreation, our sense of humor, even our mortality. Holding onto life with a white-knuckled grip allows no space for spontaneity, for discovery or possibility. This is very much a spiritual issue.

    To make space for the unpredictable allows Mystery to enter which, in turn, may provide surprising answers, new questions, remarkable healing. Then we begin to learn that there is a difference between *letting go* and *giving up*.

How often do you find yourself tightly gripping your fists or your jaw? How often do you find yourself directing the actions of others instead of looking to them for direction? When have you last rested in total space and discovered that peace which escapes our understanding?

*I know my time is short. I sense separation… red fades to brown… I must let go … How peaceful to finally let go.*

# Woman Snake

I had an image of a knotted black tie lying on my chest. But sometimes the tie would change to a coiled black snake. It was not menacing, but I had a sense of not wanting to move or I would disturb the *tie-snake*.

I lifted the snake off my chest to hold it out, looking at it more closely. I was told to throw it down on the ground. Look at it. Gain some distance from it. What kind of snake is it?

It is large – no, growing larger – a boa constrictor. I could not possibly pick it up with one hand. It is much too large for me and even if I could even get both hands around its thickness, it would envelope me, bind me, constrict me, choke me. I tell myself some people have made pets of them and allow them to be like a stole around their shoulders. I can't do that! (Funny, I was not afraid of snakes when I was a child – even taking delight in taunting my father who was afraid of snakes.)

I just can't bear the weight and the pressure. Yes, it is beautiful and powerful – more power than I would want – yet I sense there is not evil within its skin.

I look at it a long time. Now I know why it is so large! It is *motherhood*! I am holding the snake filled with all the mothers of my ancestry – the mothers who appear so perfect to me, the mothers who abuse their children, the mothers in poverty who cannot feed their children, the mothers whose children are sick and dying. I cannot bear the weight of all those mothers. I cannot be a perfect mother.

I weep for the burden of mothers contained within the skin of the boa constrictor. I weep for myself.

*(To be continued . . . )*

# Woman Snake Reflections

## Connected to the World

When God was knitted to our body in the Virgin's womb,
God took our Sensuality and oned it to our Substance
Thus our Lady is our Mother in whom we are all enclosed
and in Christ we are born of her.

We were all created at the same time;
and in our creation we were knit and oned to God.
By this we are kept as luminous and noble as when we were created,
By the force of this precious oneing we love, seek, praise, thank,
and endlessly enjoy our Creator.

Julian of Norwich, 14th century English mystic

We are never given a mystical experience to fossilize, as a seashell or insect -- for to do that would be to kill it first. We are never gifted with images of insight to hold onto selfishly though we may never share them openly with another person. Our connections with God are always given to expand our understanding of the world as well as ourselves. This particular meditation seemed to pull me right out of my skin and into the lives of many other women in a most unexpected way. What started out as a fearful image emerged as an ancient image used to portray the mystery of woman.

My experiences crossed over time and rational space to connect with those of women everywhere and anytime. In these brief moments, in this unusual image, our pain, our struggles, our conflicts, our choices converged. I had come to this prayer time seeking guidance with a vocational decision. And, in a bold move, I was patched into the wisdom of all women. My challenges were both validated and put into perspective. Through my personal experience, I became connected to a much wider reality.

Where do you connect with others? How can the collective wisdom of others who have experienced similar pain, challenge, success, failure, courage assist you? How can you foster these connections?

The snake you carry is changeable – reach out. What do you hold now? A wooden spoon!

# Woman Snake

How can motherhood be proof of my call, God?

"Look again at the snake, Jannel."

As I look again a transformation has taken place -- It is only a molted shell of the snake. What snake is there now for me? Have I lost it all?

"The snake you carry is changeable -- reach out. What do you hold now? A wooden spoon!     "Right, reach again."

A simple brass cross. (*This resembles a cross given us at our wedding.*)

"Right, motherhood, womanhood and priesthood are linked inextricably for you. You need not give up one for the other. Because you are woman you are mother -- more than just to your daughters. You are linked to all mothers. I need you to be fully woman, mother and priest to respond to my call. It is because you are all these that some will hear me through you where others could not. Carry the burden lightly."

Each one of us is called to a particular task in life. This is not just true for those in the church business. We all have particular skills, gifts, and preferences that can shape our vocation and give us satisfaction. Discerning that task, role, or job can be difficult -- especially, if we don't think we want to do what we hear asked of us. Listening for the voice of Wisdom deep within may be difficult, but it leads us to our deepest yearning. It may also help us to grow in confidence and self-worth. Listen well. It will also benefit the world.

What blocks your *call* -- or your responding to the call? What expectations -- from family, society, your experience -- cloud your decisions? How can you overcome these obstacles and find satisfaction? What images does God offer to give new meaning to your choices?

# Woman Snake Further Reflections
## Discerning the Call

Some images appear in story and song over and over again, and seem to carry the same meaning regardless of culture and personality. The interpretations of some images have shifted depending upon the commentator, but they really belong in the dictionary of universal language. Carl Jung called them archetypes, referring to the images that appear in dreams which are symbolic of life experiences.

The snake is a curious image. According to Jung, it generally represents the male/phallic symbol. Yet, here, in my experience, the snake was clearly feminine. Did I get this one wrong? I don't think so. Remember the story of Adam, Eve and the Serpent? What is not so frequently told about this story is that at the time of its writing, the neighboring goddess cults viewed the snake as very feminine. The snake was worshiped for its ability to shed skin and still live -- be reborn. Woman is able to bleed and still live -- be reborn. And of course, a woman is able to carry life within her -- bear new life. The cult was a threat to the emerging, primarily patriarchal image for God. Thus, the snake became the villain!

Upon reflection the snake bears additional meaning in this meditation. I came into this silent space seeking guidance about my being called to become a priest. There was a great deal of resistance within me because of the very male role a priest cast. I could not see how I might maintain my essential feminine nature and serve as a priest. What could I bring? How much of *me* might I lose? What effect would my job have on being a mother?

In the end, in a rather amusing way, the paradox of the priestly – primarily male – call came together with an ancient feminine image by way of God's Wisdom. The meditation continued…

# Power and Mystery

Power is Authority
> Mystery is humbling;

Power is strength
> Mystery cautions – Beware!

Power rides a dragon
> Mystery just appears;

Power is full of plans
> Mystery warns – not so fast!

Power is the ocean's wave
> Mystery is what lies beneath;

Power demands
> Mystery restores;

Power knows fear
> Mystery knows freedom;

Power can cripple
> Mystery brings comfort

Power can turn back
> Mystery nudges forward

Power is the babe
> Mystery is the secret of conception

Power embraces
> Mystery loves

Power and Mystery
> join to play fine music.

God empowers through the Spirit
> to teach the Mystery of Creation.

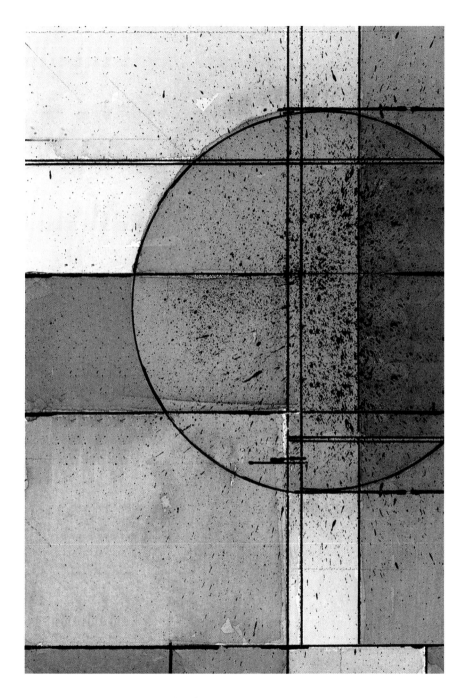

*Power and Mystery join to play fine music.*

# Power and Mystery Reflections
## Finding Balance

O that you would tear open the heavens and come down,
so that the mountains would quake at your presence… so
that the nations might tremble at your presence! When you
did awesome deeds that we did not expect, you came down.
From ages past no one has heard, no ear has perceived, no
eye has seen any God besides you, who works for those who
wait for him.

Isaiah 64:1-3, NRSV

Even before recorded history, one person made the observation and told another person. A wise one told the tribe what they had heard and it was passed down from one generation to another generation, from one people to another people. It was not limited to one part of the world, either, but seemed to begin and spread spontaneously in places around the world.

After many years of the telling, some believed it and others did not. Still the observation continued to be passed down though it changed over time. Still some believed it and other did not. Most people knew they could never full understand – still they tried. Later, scientists tried to convince people it was not true – that they could explain it all; but, the observation continued to fascinate and disturb all the people.

Finally some physicists and other scientists said it must be true, though they still could not really explain it: *there is a power so great in the universe that it must have started everything.* The Power is so great it may (for scientists *never* say anything definitively) have created the Earth. Some believed it, others did not.

Some thought they could understand the Power better if they made it human-like. So they called it *He* and imagined this Power could do everything they could not. Some tried to be as powerful as It was. Others said It's power was in its creative and re-creative energy which was too mysterious to understand. Still others said It was both too powerful and too mysterious to comprehend. Still people tried to understand because it seemed like It wanted to be understood. People reported that they could feel and see the Power. Their hearts could sense the Mystery. Still, some believed and some did not. Perhaps some must see the Power and some must feel the Mystery. Some must know *why*, others just *know*.

Still people tried to understand because it seemed like It wanted to be understood. People reported that they could feel and see the Power. Their hearts could sense the Mystery. Still, some believed and some did not. Perhaps some must see the Power and some must feel the Mystery. Some must know *why*, others just know. Some think they have to do with gender or social position or wealth or age or how the story is read and understood.

Power and Mystery are beyond human comprehension though we may get glimpses. We may try in many ways to create power or mystery for ourselves – for constructive or destructive purposes. The irony is that these glimpses usually reveal more about ourselves than about the Creator. Perhaps it is that we are an imperfect reflection. This is what has fascinated us from the beginning of time: the undeniable Power inherent in the natural world around us and the unexplainable Mystery that dwells in the most unlikely places. The tricky yet critical part for us is to accept the two as a balance.

How do you experience Mystery in your life? When has power influenced your understanding of God/Power? Why might it be important to appreciate the balance of Power and Mystery? What words would *you* use to describe Power and Mystery? What words would you use to describe Power and Mystery? What images come to mind?

# Growing in Faith

## Study
### (Or, Pondering the Possible)

Deeper reflection shows that the science of theology and the practice of prayer are closer than we ordinarily think… Theology and spirituality need one another with the unity of the Christian life.

John Macquarrie[20]

Looking back over the past twenty years of my active spiritual exploration, I can easily see my points of intellectual hunger. There was my Jungian phase. This actually was my point of re-entry into faith after years away from any formal religious expression. One wise woman suggested that dreams were the universal experience through which God could communicate. This made sense to me. I had recalled vivid dreams and intuitively knew they had to mean something for me, but I did not have the tools or the confidence to discover their meaning. So I read every book I could find on dreams. I talked with people more knowledgeable than I about dream work and interpretation. My discoveries began to give shape and form to what I had been sensing – my dreams were another connection with God. I dreamed, recorded my dreams in a journal, read about dreams and interpretation of dreams and dreamed some more until I was exhausted. I was exhausted, but also exhilarated to realize that I was part of a much bigger system – a whole community of dreamers from all time and all cultures. I had also found a new way to expand my relationship with God which helped me bring my life into better focus.

From that study and reflection on my experiences, I was able to understand God to be much bigger than I had ever known before. I discovered that God has spoken to unnumbered people throughout time, across artificial boundaries such as cultures or religious tenets, through their dreams. This bigger God was the One I could embrace. By taking the time to consider the writings of others, I had grown spiritually. I was no longer hindered in my faith by the limited resources of my Sunday school education. I was encouraged by these first hesitant steps into the study of spirituality to continue exploring other areas. My world had opened up. My mind began to work in more conscious cooperation with my heart. This little taste of knowledge made me yearn for more and follow the paths my yearning took me. Each path I followed seemed to open onto another.

Next came my exploration into the "spiritual disciplines." I read and studied many books on the subject, ancient and modern. I attended classes and conferences and began to incorporate the practices into my life. In a similar way, when my feminine awareness was awakened, I read about women's ways of knowing God and self. I read about goddesses, women in myths, women in history, women in the Bible, and devoured the plethora of feminist literature which was emerging. There was my creation-centered phase, in which I discovered that we could choose to believe we were born in sin or created in love. I researched the models of spiritual and emotional development, in an attempt to get a sense of where I was on this complex path on which I had launched myself. I read more and more about ways to pray and live the spiritual life. All this took place before I went to seminary. My formal theological education provided all kinds of material to sort through, to critique, to incorporate into my life or toss out, to clarify my faith or confuse me. As I studied more and more about prayer and the experiences others have had with God, I found validation as well as insight for my own experiences. I was drawn to the writings of the medieval women mystics who were so open, loving and creative in their prayer experiences, yet thoughtful and grounded in the teachings of the church. They were strong, influential women who talked about God in ways that I could understand.

Each hunger marked a stage of yearning for me to know more about how others have understood God which, in turn, helped me define my own understanding. The discipline of study have deepened my spiritual life, challenged my easy and popular assumptions, broadened my understanding of the Christian tradition, and expanded my appreciation of other faiths. At the same time, I discovered a clearer focus of what is important to my own beliefs. In addition to the reading, I also made time to think, examine ideas with others, reject some parts, claim other parts, integrate what is appropriate and let go of those things which do not fit.

Study is another tool, a spiritual discipline, that we have available to deepen our life in the spirit. We cannot separate heart from head, our emotions from our intellect. We must nurture both and seek ways to make sense out of our thoughts through experience and our experiences through thoughtful reflection. Study can move us out of self-absorption. It can rescue us from the trap of becoming self-satisfied, arrogant that we have it all right and figured out. Reading the insights of others or the history of a certain tradition can open possibilities for a more mature faith and for growing more fully into relationship with Holy Wisdom.

The experience of soaring to the sun on the back of Mother Dolphin was just a wonderful feeling, an imaginative experience, for a long time. I could not quite sort out what instruction it held for me, though I had come to associate the Holy Spirit very clearly with this creature of water and air. Then I read about the symbolism attributed to the sun in mythic literature outside western culture. In many traditions the sun symbolizes hope and illumination. One of the most important symbols, the sun also represents warmth, joy and inspiration. This experience of being transported by "The Spirit" may well have been my internal preparation for the writing of this book. This creation would require deep, focused communication between heart and head as well as all the inspiration – and hope – I could get.

As in all the disciplines, there are pitfalls. If we fall in love with the discipline itself and fail to see it as a guide, we may find ourselves trapped in a corner of *the corral*! Or we may discover we are racing from one interest or conference to another, one good idea to another good idea, one insight to another, without taking the time to integrate what we have learned – or even making a conscious decision that it is worth integrating. It may also be a sign that we are avoiding something much more important that lies within us. Too much of any one thing can either restrict us or send us off on the wrong path. When used well, the discipline of study enhances and opens our comprehension. Some things to beware:

- We can become too reliant on others' opinions and neglect listening carefully to and acknowledging the wisdom of our inner voice. Learning to say *no* to what does not ring true and to say *yes* to what does can save us from riding a popular bandwagon too far afield.

- We may be tempted to replace study for silence or prayer. Words are very seductive, especially when they are said so cleverly and so much better by an expert.

- We could place so much emphasis on study that we limit our really living into our insights and learnings. They remain cerebral abstractions, interesting points or excellent logic, which separate instead of connect us to God.

- We may be tempted to take things too literally. Any writing must be approached with an attitude of questioning, recalling, for instance, that history can be written from a ruler's perspective or from the woman on the street; an economist's viewpoint or a migrant worker's; a man's angle or a child's. The perspective shades the interpretation and therefore, the"truth." We must even be careful to know about the Bible we use. Is it a careful translation, or is it a person's interpretation or version?

Study is really the exercise step in our faith development. It helps to shape the relationship we are trying to establish with the Holy One. Study assists us in more clearly comprehending the framework of the faith we choose. If we do not take time to think through the ideas that are embedded in the assumptions of a faith story, we may find ourselves lost when we need it most. If we do not actively engage our intellect, we may discover a shaky framework, upon which we are building our spiritual life. Study helps us discover both flaws and gifts. At the very least, it helps us discover for ourselves what fits for us. Study is really the excercise of reflecting upon our experiences or the experiences of others. It allows us to gain perspective on our actions and assumptions. We then are able to change where necessary and become more grounded where we already are. Study helps us grow out of our Sunday school assumptions and into mature faith. Sometimes this means we must wrestle with what is comfortable but limiting and what is challenging but enlivening. Whether we read books, examine scripture, seek insight from the arts or carefully observe the world around us, study enables us to throw open the gates of narrow assumption and ponder the possible – even our relationship with God.

# Guidance
## (Or, We Can't Do It Alone)

Spiritual direction takes up the concrete daily experiences of our lives and gives them sacramental significance.[21]

Richard J. Foster

It is an ancient tradition in all cultures for a wise one – mentor, guru, rabbi, spiritual director, teacher, crone, a more experienced traveler – to guide others along their spiritual way. They encourage, challenge, correct, instruct. Mostly, they listen. They provide models for faithfulness, and they hold the disciple accountable. Styles of direction or guidance may vary depending upon the tradition from which we come. Sometimes a single individual will act as guide. At other times, it may be the entire community with its years of tradition that serves that function.

A very homely image comes to me to describe the kind of relationship I have in mind. Our daughters were excited to bring home a new hamster. They put it on the bed to watch it run around, frightened and unsure of its surroundings and boundaries. Our dog, an Australian sheep dog, came to the rescue. True to her nature and breeding, she responded to the crisis. Very calmly, she moved around the bed, nudging the hamster back on whenever it came close to running right off the bed. Spiritual guides are something like that!

I have had several gifted women and men guide me at different times in my life. Some people are able to find one person to act as guide for most of their life. I have also had individuals who have offered guidance in other ways, more like spiritual friends. Sometimes, a group can serve the same purpose of nudging us back to where we need to be.

Guidance may come from any place – an offhand remark from a stranger, a painting or photograph, a piece of music, a loved one, a book, a sermon or presentation, or a children's story. However, there is a real benefit from being committed to an on-going relationship with someone who is trained, experienced and who sees the changes and patterns in us. I recall asking my physician if she thought yearly physicals were really helpful. (There had been an article in the news saying they were a waste of time.) She said they could be a waste of time if you saw a new doctor every time. The benefit of a yearly physical examination is in seeing the changes over time. She knows me and knows when something in particular needs attention. She knows what I respond to most effectively and those things that are injurious to my health. In the same way, a spiritual director or guide knows the journey we have been on, the relationships we have with other people, our gifts and our weaknesses, where we have matured and where growth is needed.

Good spiritual directors will hold our feet on the path and our hearts to the purpose. They help us remain focused on what is central, assisting us in casting aside those things which inhibit or distract us. They help us discern whether our decisions and actions are life-giving or robbing us of true freedom. They enable us to interpret what is happening to us in a larger perspective, so we do not get caught in the minutiae of excuses and circumstances. They may stimulate our imagination and offer possibilities. They help us make the connections between the state of our spiritual lives and the way we are living and loving at home and in the world. They provide a safe place to express our doubts, confess our sins, and test out new insights. They assist us in seeing God where we were otherwise blind.

Finding one may be difficult, depending upon the part of the country in which you live. The best thing to do is to ask people you respect and who have experienced such guidance. You may find assistance also through local religious houses or retreat centers. In his book, *Spiritual Friend*, Tilden Edwards presents a good history of spiritual direction and guidelines for choosing a director and for being in direction.[22] Also, Richard Foster's book, *Celebration of Discipline,* includes an excellent chapter on direction, both individual and corporate.

After nearly twenty years of meditating on the first image that I described in this book, *Mother Earth,* and finding no really satisfying interpretation, I presented it to my director for help. In the process of asking me just a few questions, she was able to tease out its previously hidden significance for me. (Spiritual direction also serves the purpose of keeping us humble, for often we miss the most obvious gift or solution presented to us.) The tomb-like space into which I was lowered below the surface of the earth was never frightening to me, though my thinking limited me to a death analogy. Yet that interpretation never felt right. The feelings I recalled were ones of comfort and security. It became clear through our conversation that I had known and felt a deep connection with the earth. Mother Earth had held me – embraced me.[23] Since my prayer had been, *Lord, let me feel your love*, I was stunned by the new understanding so long after the experience.  It also made sense in the way it had *grounded* me in a creation-centered understanding of the Divine.

Sometimes, a spiritual guide will notice patterns of behavior that are not healthy and may present roadblocks on the spiritual path. Such behavior may foster ill health, create or sustain destructive relationships, or limit our natural abilities. In these cases, it is very important for the spiritual director to help the directee discover a process for healing, or perhaps refer him to a counselor or therapist. The work of the spiritual director is one of enabling the person to draw closer to God, clarifying his life in light of his faith and helping him discover how that might be lived in the world. More serious personality work must be left to the therapist. However, it may be possible, and in fact, advisable, to work with both spiritual director and counselor. If spiritual issues continue to arise, the director may be able to encourage hope and provide support to the work that is being done in therapy.

There are also times in our lives when a small group can be of great help in discerning the Spirit and helping to clarify a decision or issue. During the time I was being considered for a new position, I called together a *circle of women* to help pray me through the transition. I was looking for honest, challenging, prayerful support of whatever decision I finally made. I very purposefully invited four women friends with different backgrounds: a good friend and deacon, a lay professional who had known me a very long time, a minister from another denomination and a new friend and educator. Each brought her own unique perspective and gifts. I asked that they offer total honesty and, for this period of time, only focus on my transition. This was the hardest part, because it felt very self-centered. I also asked for a commitment to meet once a month until a decision was made. The stated purpose was to help me gain clarity in my commitment for the future – whatever that might be.

Each time we met, I took a few minutes to bring them up-to-date on the events that had taken place since our last meeting, without much discussion. I might present a question that was haunting me or ask for feedback on something that I had said or done. Each time one of us was designated to offer a prayer, an image, a poem or piece of writing that she thought appropriate. We would sit in silence in my prayer room at home for as much time as we needed. No one watched the clock. At the end of the time, each would offer whatever image or comment came to her in the silence for my guidance. Sometimes there would be discussion. Other times, I would listen to the offering to consider later. They never failed to give me just what I needed to hear. In this "group guidance" they enabled me to move into and through a significant transition. This short term direction was just what I needed at the time.[24]

Anyone who is serious about pursuing her spiritual life with the Holy must eventually find a guide. Of course, the guide is only as helpful as our willingness to commit to the discipline and to risk moving in new directions, as well as making ourselves vulnerable to honest reflection. The way to God is perilous if we think we can travel it strictly through our own willfulness. Teresa of Avila warns serious souls of the reptiles or vermin which lurk at the gates of our *Interior Castle* – the place where we truly find God – preventing us from seeing the beauty of the castle, and coming to know the true blessing and love of God for us.[25] A guide can make us aware of those things which block our way or attack us in order to keep us from coming to know God's love completely.

# Ritual
## (Or, Moving the Inside Outside)

Love, whether of God or of the girl [boy] next door, is all but impossible to express except through outward symbolic action, that is, through ritual acts.[26]

Leonel L. Mitchell

In retrospect, I think I became ordained – at least partially – because I so appreciate ritual. Please don't misunderstand me. I do not mean mindless repetition or thoughtless attempts to express every emotion publicly. I understand ritual to be a spiritual discipline which can guide and open us to deeper understanding of ourselves and the Mystery of God by acting out, in some way, what we may not otherwise adequately express only in words. I have included ritual in this section on *Growing in Faith* because we learn and grow through all our senses. Ritual engages our bodies, stimulates our imaginations, and stretches our capacity to see God in new ways. Rituals can express what we feel inside, even if we don't realize we feel it. Rituals also offer the opportunity to be connected with others in expressions of faith and tradition. Community life is an integral part of the Christian life. That is, shared faith enables, enhances and deepens individual experiences of faith. Rituals are another means for making this happen, even if it means merely sitting together in silence. When we express what we feel or believe outwardly, it somehow gives validation and reality to that which we cannot name easily. It brings Mystery to life!

In my church tradition, ritual is highly regarded. I fear at times it is worshiped for its own sake and not for what it represents and makes possible; however, time and again I have seen how this discipline of acting out prayer moves people to deeper faith. This is the mystery inherent in it. Rituals engage the senses and awakens memories and insights in surprising ways which we might not have expected. Rituals can manifest what is only hinted at in our awareness, using symbols to express many levels of meaning. Rituals can engage long standing traditions which link people across time, or they can be created for a special occasion. Rituals can be familiar repetition or creative expression of old traditions. Rituals can bring people together to across cultural and political barriers. Rituals bridge language gaps and age differences as little else can.

An individual can also benefit from moving through a rhythm of prayer and action that expresses a spiritual dilemma. The sacrament of confession or reconciliation is one ancient way for individuals to seek resolution to brokenness in their lives. Sometimes a particular occasion requires the formation of a new ritual. A woman had been coming to me for spiritual direction for some time. She was wrestling with unhealthy, past relationships with men and her desire to be in relationship with God. She seemed to be really stuck – feeling guilty, used, conned, and left. While she could identify all these feelings, she could not seem to let go of them. I suggested she might take paper and pastel crayons, put some music on that suited her mood and draw what she felt. She did this several times. Through the act of drawing and the insights the drawings provided her she gained a new measure of freedom from her past, but it still was not fully resolved for her. So I invited her to think of a way she might make her healing more visible or real through a simple ritual. She came the next time with her drawings, some prayers, and some matches. We went to the church courtyard. I joined her in the reciting of the prayers and witnessed her confession of compliance and reassured her of God's love and forgiveness for her. She put the pictures on the ground, set fire to them and watched them burn. We stood in silence for several moments. Then, I stepped on the ashes. She immediately took over, stepping – or stomping! – on all the ashes. Before long we were both laughing and crying. All the serious talking or "processing" in the world would not have brought her to that point of release.

The rational becomes non-rational. Time is compressed or expanded to accommodate the inner need. Ritual invites Mystery in because we don't have to give it words which limit our full expression. Mystery transforms the ordinary into the extraordinary. Mystery touches our very soul and we are changed. It can happen alone with the simple lighting of a candle to mark the beginning of a time of meditation. It can happen with many people present, rehearsing old customs or creating new ones, sharing a meal, singing or playing music, reciting ancient texts or developing new language to express the group experience and need. Ritual can mean sitting quietly in a prescribed place, or it can be active body movement – running, walking, dancing, swaying or stomping. In all these activities, what makes it ritual is not just repeating the activity It is becoming conscious and attentive to the presence of God in the midst of activity. Body, mind and spirit are linked together through ritual.

Central to my spirituality is the ritual of Holy Communion or Holy Eucharist, eating a little piece of bread and drinking a sip of wine in the context of a community gathered together. These common elements take on deep symbolism for the body and blood of Jesus Christ and his deep, sacrificing love for all people. The symbols of this ritual are filled with many levels of meaning. We act out this ritual every week, because we can never fully plumb the depths of meaning that this act contains. It is the core of our faith to which we return each week to become connected – to ourselves, to the people in our community and to God. This ritual of scripture and a symbolic meal unites the community – the present body of Christ – with the mystical Christ. We are then sent out into our little piece of the world to act out the life of faith, the values taught and the love given to be shared. Sometimes, we forget to remember the significance. Any ritual is prone to acting out mere motions if not offered carefully and mindfully. Yet its repetition also makes available, at any moment, the possibility of God breaking through the familiar and ordinary act of a simple meal making it extraordinary.

One time, after a funeral, a woman approached me. She said it was the first time she had experienced communion led by a woman. This ritual was very familiar to her, but my presence as a woman priest had changed her experience of God. She described it as "watching me cook up some eucharist at the table." I recalled this description when I looked once again at *The Snake* encounter I had had so many years before. Maybe a wooden spoon is just the thing when you are "cooking up" eucharist and making ritual. What contains more ritual than family celebrations around a meal and what experience contains more levels of meaning?

Some rituals are meant to meet the needs of the moment. Others attain such rich, deep meaning that no matter how often they are performed, they continue to touch and stretch and inspire individuals to grow in faith. Often, the mere fact that individuals come together in the shared experience is enough to create the space needed for the Spirit to break in. Then as with all the other disciplines, we must take our experience out into the places we live, enriched and strengthened. This means that we are better able to live our lives centered on God, better connected to ourselves and to each other.

*Growing in Faith* is an attitude toward living which allows us to stretch our limits, push back our preconceived notions and open up possibilities for change, which may then draw us closer to God. *Growing in Faith* is the meat and substance of who we are now as well as our potential for who we might become. The disciplines of study, guidance and ritual offer opportunities to flex our spiritual muscles of intellect and real muscles of the body. These disciplines move us out of a solitary experience of the Holy and into the company of other believers. This is good, because we might become tempted to think that we have all the answers and know God well enough on our own. We shall never know God well enough!

*Study* is one way to ponder what might be possible. This discipline can be stimulating and energizing for the pure joy of engaging our intellect. We can also delight in what another person has discovered, especially if she is able to say clearly something about which we have only had an inkling. Typically, we get so excited about it, we buy the book or copy the article and pass it on to a friend. When we uncover a truth or a pattern to which both our mind and our heart say, Yes! we can rejoice in discovering a new tool of enlightenment – and, perhaps, it changes our life.

Like growth experiences, we need some kind of guide. We needed our parents or siblings to prop us up as we learned to walk. Or they knelt three steps ahead of us, smiling and urging us forward. Teachers, coaches and pastors gave us new information, corrected our mistakes and opened vistas for us. The discipline of *guidance* is understanding that we do not need to travel the spiritual road alone. Another person may be able to point out the signs along the way that could save our walking the long way round – or off the cliff.

The discipline of *ritual* allows us an opportunity to share our faith with others. What we have come to know within us, we can bring to the light by engaging our whole being. When we participate in sacramental rituals with others, we may discover new, very personal insights which are life-changing. Outward symbolic actions knit us together – mind, body and soul. They transform us and help us grow in faith.

# Ocean Flight

[One moment I was sitting in the room in silence with others. We focused on a candle in the middle of the room. I closed my eyes and knew that I had moved deep within myself. I returned to a familiar centering place – a rock in the watery depths of my internal ocean…]

A large gray dolphin swam toward me…

This meeting seemed as natural as my being able

to breath easily miles beneath the surface of water.

We looked at each other for a long time, then

she invited me to ride on her back.

I climbed on and we swam together as one,

deep in the waters of my inner self.

But, after some time, this space became too confining

so we swam out into wider water, the ocean,

and emerged on the surface.

We swam together as if we had done it a thousand times.

I felt safe -- exhilarated – alive.

Other dolphins joined us.

I asked my dolphin's name – *Mother Dolphin* – she told me.

We swam far out in the ocean

marking no time or distance.

I spoke to her again and asked if she could fly…

[What made me do such a thing?]

*… we swam together as one, deep in the waters of my inner self.*

# Ocean Flight Reflections
## Awakening

The Holy Spirit is a Burning Spirit, Who kindles the hearts of humankind,
playing them like tympanum and lyre,
gathering volume in the temple of the soul.

The Holy Spirit is Life-giving-life, all movement, root of all being,
purifier of all impurity, absolver of all faults, balm of all wounds,
radiant life, worthy of all praise.
The Holy Spirit resurrects and awakens everything that is.

Hildegard of Bingen, 12th century German mystic

How many of us go about our days putting one foot in front of the other? How many of us complain, whine, grouse about this or that, but make no move to change us or what annoys us? How many of us have read the same words to prayers week after week without any sense of what they are saying? How many of us long for insight into a dilemma, but can't seem to move past our predictable, routine responses? I would venture to say — all of us, at some time or another.

We fall asleep at the wheel of life and start to drift off into numbness. This is not what living is about. We have only to watch nature for a season or two to discover that life is full of *awakenings*. The same is true in the life of the Spirit.

Had I "fallen asleep" or gone too deep within myself? Had I become too focused on my own needs? In order to see life with fresh perspective, to truly change, we *must* dive deeply within ourselves first. There is a danger, however, in finding the internal spot so familiar and comfortable that we become unwilling to venture out – to really live into the change.

If we remain attentive, the Spirit may then draw us out and awaken our senses enlivening us – from the inside out. Practically speaking, this can happen in many different ways — as simply as the comment of a child or as dramatically as illness or death. We all need to be awakened from time to time so that we may appreciate life anew, incorporate changes, and become truer to ourselves. This is not only good for us, but also important for those around us.

When is the last time you remember "falling asleep" on life or becoming too self-absorbed that you lost perspective? What awakened you? What effect did that process have on you? on those you love? those you work with?

# Sun Flight

She said, yes… we leaped together as we had in the waves

but, now only air surrounded us.

As if they were made of some firm substance,

we swam on the sun's beams.

Higher and higher we flew,

undulating as one,

yet, always flying higher.

In no time – or in all time – we reached the sun.

I told her I was hungry.

*Mother Dolphin* instructed me to break off a piece

of the sun and eat it.

So I reached out and broke off a chunk.

I offered some to her and we ate together.

It tasted like honey and wild fresh wind.

As we flew back toward the earth,

I carried a piece of the leftover sun back with me.

I held it in my hands – warm and glowing

and brought it back to my inner self

letting it rest there,

saving it to share with someone else sometime.

*We swam on the sun's beams... higher and higher we flew... until we reach the sun.*

# Sun Flight Reflections

## Imagination

"But that's your imagination!"
"Of course, what else can God use?"

Taken from *Joan of Arc*, by George Bernard Shaw

The Holy Spirit expresses the imagination of God. Imagination is the gift of no oughts or shoulds, no rules or limitations -- only possibilities. You might caution me to say imagination can be and has been used for evil purposes. That is true. This is imagination in the absence of love. For the most part, western culture discourages using our imaginations -- except for the crazy and wild inventors, artists and children. We expect that they will use their imaginations, but we *ordinary* mature adults are much too sophisticated, informed and realistic – or – inhibited to set our imaginations free.

Most of us were told in grade school that we could not draw -- that is we could not reproduce real things to look real. We were discouraged from writing poetry -- except as an assignment which was graded. We were directed toward a profession that would earn us a good living -- which generally means lacking in imagination but predictable, safe and familiar.

Perhaps you are thinking that my imagination has run more than wild and I am justifying it by calling it *mystical!* Perhaps you are right. But what better proof of God?

We need imagination to pray. We need imagination to — well, imagine the possible solutions to a dilemma. It is imagination that can save us from depression, provide courage when we lack it most or help us meet our deepest selves most constructively. Imagination is the essential ingredient in creativity. God must have a great imagination given the variety and scope of creation!

When is the last time you let your imagination carry you away? Who has discouraged you from using it? How has your ability to imagine opened possibilities for you? What have you been taught about God and imagination?

# A Psalm: Fire and Spirit

The water is good inside and healing
　　　and the flame is energy,
　　　　　and somehow, somewhere –
the dark clay pot that covered the flame has been overturned.
　　　Now it is like a kettle holding glowing coals.
Like the center of the earth –
　　　the same core of fiery energy that fuels the earth.
　　　It is a piece of the first fire that blazed in the cosmos
　　　　　and it rests within this woman – me.
The water and the flame are part of me just as they are the earth.
　　　I am earth's child.
　　　　　I am mystery.
　　　　　　　I am fragile, yet resilient.
You are there, Great God, in the flame –
　　　in the cave of my fiery passion,
　　　　　in my little girl flame – in my darkness.
You are there, Mother God,
　　　in my watery womb
　　　　　in the birth and rebirth of my soul.
You are there, ruah God.
　　　In the gold glow you fan the flame to greater intensity.
　　　Like the flames of Pentecost
　　　　　you blow across time and space
　　　　　　　ignoring obstacles,
　　　　　　　　　whistling through vulnerable apertures
　　　　　　　　　　　making music as on a flute.
You, O Mother Wind,
　　　give flight to fragile wings
　　　　　taking them where all is bright.
Fly me, Powerful One.
　　　Take me beyond myself –
　　　　　beyond the insulation of my flesh
　　　　　　　that dampens my flame,
　　　　　　　　　that retards the glow so others might see.
Fly me, Spirit of Life,
　　　and expand my horizons –
　　　　　show me new places.
Bless me, Origin of All,
　　　that I may swim and fly in your creation
　　　　　forever.

*The water is good inside and healing… The flame is energy… now a kettle holding glowing coals… The water and the flame…*

# Fire and Spirit Reflections
## Passion

Earth is crammed with heaven,
>     And every common bush afire with God.
But only they who see take off their shoes.
>     The rest just sit around and pluck blackberries.[27]

Elizabeth Barrett Browning, 19th century English poet

I recall a time in my life when I got very confused about the accusation that I was an angry woman. I searched my soul. I agonized about having been rude or cruel. I thought a great deal about what I had been taught about being angry -- basically, don't be! I wanted to take seriously the "critique," but I could not sort it out or make it fit with how I felt. What would make these people think I was angry?

Three years later, I once again was confronted with the observation that I was still being angry -- though they could not identify particular outbursts or examples of angry encounters. One person said it was my eyes -- or my facial expressions -- something about me that felt intense. While I was much more comfortable with myself by this time, I was still confused.

Finally, one person exclaimed, "I know what it is! It is PASSION!."

Aha! That rang true. Strong emotion. Intense feelings, thoughts, beliefs. Deep commitment. Passion goes against the cultural grain of being "cool." It is a close neighbor to anger and can swing over quickly, but it is not synonymous with anger. Mostly, we think of passion in relation to lust or craving but that is much too limiting. Passion is exciting, energizing, motivating. Like anything, it can be carried too far, but passion stirs the soul and awakens the slumbering spirit. It moves us into action, and it may move others.

What makes you feel passionate, stirs up your blood? When might your emotions have been misunderstood?  How do you express your passion -- with quiet commitment, wearing it on your sleeve, unexpressed? When have you been discouraged from feeling or expressing strong emotions?

# The Tree

I felt like I was on an elevator in a rapid descent below the surface of the earth. Jesus was with me as I got off and I found myself in a tunnel of earth. At first I was a little frightened, but I felt him take my hand. We walked deeper and deeper into the earth and I was surprised at how much air there was. It was dark, loamy, rich earth.

We sat together for a time in a little *pocket* of air. I don't know how far down we were, but it was very dark, yet I could see. I asked him what we were doing here. He said, "You will grow." I thought about the little seeds that, just a few moments before (in real time), I had planted in my margarine containers in the laundry room. I always doubt that such little things could survive and grow and produce the fruit for which I hope. I felt a curious kinship with them. I imagined their roots beginning to reach out into the soil and moisture. I thought about the curly willow and its rapid growing fine white roots and then, *I* began to grow!

I could feel my finger tips and toes literally tingling. They seemed to be sprouting the beginnings of thin white roots. Once begun, like time-lapse photography, the roots grew and grew – branching off and spreading out through the earth. My fingers and toes continue to tingle.

Then, my neck curved and suddenly I was popping into the light, stretching my neck, and torso toward the sun becoming tall and slender. My hair started to tingle and each strand became a branch with tender, small light green leaves. The wind blew and I could feel the leaves moving but not being blown off.

I stopped the rapid growth and looked at myself. I had smooth bark. What kind of tree was I – maybe a birch or a curly willow or a paloverde – but, it was no use. I was like no other tree. I breathed in the fresh air and was content to be my own tree.

*… then, I began to grow.  I could feel my finger tips and toes literally tingling… sprouting thin white roots… Then my neck curved and, suddenly, I was popping into the light… torso toward the sun… The wind blew and I could feel the leaves move. I was like no other tree.*

# The Tree Reflections
## Connecting to Earth

[When] you walk along a country road and notice a little tuft of grass… the next time you pass that way you must stop to see how it is getting along and how much it has grown.

Georgia O'Keeffe (1887-1986)


To those who have not yet learned the secret of true happiness, begin now to study the little things in your own door yard.

George Washington Carver (1864-1943)


One touch of nature makes the whole world kin.

William Shakespeare (1564-1616)


I do not know whether I was then a man dreaming I was a butterfly, or whether I am now a butterfly dreaming I am a man.

Chuang Tzu (369-286 B.C.)[28]

Many people say that they find God in nature. What a good place to discover God -- in the very mystery of Creation! Who has not been awe-struck by a sunset that makes us *feel* pink? Who has not marveled at the power of the ocean's waves making and re-making the shoreline? What adult can deny a childlike thrill when we see the first pale green shoots of slumbering tulip bulbs or peonies that emerge in spring? Who is not fascinated by the simple beauty of a cardinal couple perched on naked winter branches? Can anyone deny the raw strength and sovereignty of flood or hurricane or volcano?

Every step we take into nature presents the possibility of encountering the Creator. And in turn, like all mystical experience, we risk encountering our self in a new way for we are as much a part of the created order as the ancient rocks or a summer shower.

When have you last walked slowly, mindfully in the woods? When have you listened to waves or felt the wind on your face? How closely have you experienced creation first hand? When has creation reached out to you? What is a powerful memory of your stepping into God's creation?

# *Living from the Center*

## *Commitment*
### *(Or, Staying Long Enough to Change)*

Our experiences in relation to commitment constitute in large part our vantage point for understanding God's commitment to us and God's desire for commitment from us… Commitment, then, entails a new relation in the *present* -- a relation of binding and being-bound, giving and being-claimed. But commitment points to the *future.*

Margaret Farley[29]

Though *commitment* is not mentioned in classical literature as one of the basic spiritual disciplines, I think in our time, it is essential to include it. Making and keeping commitments is part of the spiritual journey. It requires our living honestly from the center of our being, and our willingness to discover and give our truest self to another. It means living a life willing to risk our most vulnerable selves by putting trust in another person or group. The challenge is staying in the commitment long enough, risking enough, trusting enough to live into our truest self while making room for someone else. The inevitable result of such a bold move is change. This is true for any commitments: marriage, friendships, religious community, partnerships, values and ideas, as well as our relationship with God. In fact, how we experience and live out our commitments in our everyday existence directly affects the kind of commitment or relationship we have with God.

In today's society we are skeptical of believing that any vow could be kept for a lifetime. How rare a Golden Anniversary will be in twenty years! In the past, the notion of being committed to a person or group (generally only marriage or religious order) by late adolescence was taken for granted. The promises that were made then defined the person's role in life and the expectations society had from them. Today, we have many more choices and fewer explicitly prescribed expectations. Young couples marry later in life; elders remarry well into their eighties. Careers have redefined traditional roles. Fewer women and men are entering professed religious communities. More people are opting for a single lifestyle. Divorce is much easier now and carries less stigma. Family units are shaped and reshaped. Membership in churches requires less, and fewer people grow up with the assumption that they will go to church at all. Yet I think there is still a deep desire in our heart of hearts to make some kind of commitment – in a very real sense, to *belong*, to be connected.

In his article, *Making a Way*, Michael Downey captures the big picture of commitment. "It is not that people today cannot make commitments. It is rather, more a matter of finding or making ways of giving expression to what makes us go on living. Our commitments are our ways of making good on life. They are ways of expressing, of naming what and whom we live for. In and through our commitments we make a way through life. We give shape to our living. Our commitments express our sense of the highest values we perceive and pursue." [30]

To make and to keep a commitment is one way we grow, change and become more genuine. Commitments make us accountable, invite us to less selfish behavior, draw us into expectations which force us to make choices and, therefore, clarify our values. Scripture grounds us in the stories of God establishing a personal relationship with the Israelites in the form of a covenant. The covenant is later ratified and reestablished in Jesus Christ who requires that we not only love God, love ourselves, but also love others.

Making a commitment moves us out of a private, insular position in life to a more public, social place. I always tell couples who come for premarital counseling that they are about to *go public* with their love. For many young couples that means helping them understand that they can no longer hide out, thinking that what they do does not affect anyone else. It does. After the promises are made and the reception flowers have wilted – even before the honeymoon begins – their relationship will change. They begin to live into the expectations already inherent in their experiences or imposed by family traditions – explicit and implicit. They are also stretched to view themselves differently, because others view them differently. At the very least, it is not so easy just to pack up and move out when things get tough. Making promises meant to last the rest of two lives is an awesome act of courage!

Sometimes, however, the marriage promises are broken, and the commitment must be ended. Two people draw apart for many reasons. Perhaps they were not living their most authentic self from the beginning, and when it begins to emerge, the other is confused and cannot reconcile the difference. There are hurt feelings, pain, anger, guilt, disillusionment -- all the stuff that makes us want to run. The discipline of commitment does not require one to stay in an already broken relationship, but it encourages one not to leave easily. Broken commitments are not limited to marriage. The same pattern can be applied to any covenantal relationship.

While the commitment of marriage comes to mind most readily, I believe there are several other ways to live into this discipline. Another traditional covenant is one made to a *community*. The reason I place community under the heading of commitment, rather than in a category all its own, is because too often we see ourselves *associated* with a community rather than *committed* to a community. There is a big difference. When we join a church, for instance, we make choices about how to be part of that community. If we only become *associated*, we would not take weekly worship very seriously. We probably would not be able or interested in finding out what this church stands for or what doctrine shapes its life. We would not come to know the lives of others in the community or care what happens to them. If, on the other hand, we decided to make a commitment to a church community, we would be concerned about how to fit into its assumptions about God, its role in society, its expectations of its members, and how we might contribute to the health of the community. We would have to take the risk, that by becoming part of this community, we might have to change our ideas about God or our understanding of people -- or ourself.

The biggest risk of all in making a commitment is that through the involvement and reflection of another or others, we might discover something new about ourselves. When we live honestly into our commitments we cannot help but be stretched, challenged, pushed and pulled out of our comfortable assumptions about who we are. Even, and perhaps more especially, the broken commitments reveal our strengths and weaknesses. Risky as making commitments might be, it is in our nature to seek them. To avoid or deny commitment is to rob us of the chance to become more fully human and more truly ourselves. To enter into commitments with an open heart and mind is to establish the willingness to grow and mature. In order to express any integrity in our lives, to make and to hold fast to clear values and authentic living, we need others to hold us accountable. The fact is we do not live in isolation and we cannot exist as if we do.

This is not only true for the social, psychological and intellectual aspects of ourselves, but it is even more so for our spiritual selves. In order to grow and mature in our understanding of God, of God's relationship to the world and our relationship with God, we must make the initial commitment to *be* in relationship with God. Then, as with every other commitment we make, we will discover ourselves more fully.

I am not the first to acknowledge this truth, by any stretch. Evelyn Underhill, the 19th century "non-mystic" (for she makes no claim to such a title; yet her definitive book, *Mysticism*, would suggest her deep communion with the Holy!) says it so well:

> "[W]e are essentially spiritual as well as natural creatures; and that therefore life in its fullness, the life that develops and uses all our capacities and fulfills all our possibilities, must involve correspondence not only with our visible and ever-changing, but also with our invisible, and unchanging environment: the Spirit of all spirits, God, in whom we live and move and have our being. The significance, the greatness of humanity, consists in our ability to do this. The meaning of our life is bound up with the meaning of the universe… For a spiritual life is simply a life in which all that we do comes from the centre, where we are anchored in God."[31]

All commitments involve risk, trust and change. To enter them in the first place is the greatest risk of all. Will he leave his socks all over the floor? Will she make me change my friends? How much will I have to give up? Will I be able to love the same person the rest of my life? So few have. Is this the right place for me? Will this relationship be like the last? So many worries hold us back from making a commitment. We may move from one relationship to another, never staying long enough to go deeply into one. That would require trust.

To trust another human being with our heart is a serious matter. To return the favor is equally serious. Is it any easier to trust God with our hearts, when we have learned how to guard them so carefully through experience? We pay a high price for the lack of trust in a person or God, because then we lose the opportunity to discover and trust ourselves. To trust another is to allow a mirror to be held up before our face, so that we can decide how we might become a better self, a healthier person.

When we are born and when we die are the only perfect times in our lives. All the time in the middle is spent trying to recover our perfect creation. Change is the stuff of the middle. Nothing in nature remains the same, even if the adaptations take centuries. Change is inevitable. Risking a commitment and learning to trust can enable us to grow through the inevitable changes of life. The mystical way is deeply connected to this pattern of risk, trust and change. It is the only way we can move closer and closer to our center, closer to God, and closer to the ones we love.

# Cosmic Awareness
## (Or, Coming to Know Our Place)

At your command all things came to be: the vast expanse of interstellar space, galaxies, suns, the planets in their courses, and this fragile earth, our island home. From the primal elements you brought forth the human race, and blessed us with memory, reason, and skill. You made us the rulers of creation, But we turned against you, and betrayed your trust; and we turned against one another.[32]

The Book of Common Prayer

What if -- for a few moments -- we could place our bare feet on the soil and allow ourselves to grow roots deep into the earth? What if we could draw nourishment from the earth, as any plant or tree can? What if we could stretch ourselves tall enough to touch the sun with our finger tips and look out over all the continents? What if we could feel the energy of the solar system course through our body as it meets the deep-rootedness of strong tendrils, buried in Mother Earth? Then we could step back to our former self. What would we be like? How would we act?

Cosmic Awareness is becoming aware of the grand scheme of the universe, and at the same time, sensitive to the microcosmic life that holds it together. Cosmic Awareness is being attentive to this *fragile earth, our island home* and the responsibility we have been given to care for it. It is seeing and feeling the connection with other persons on this planet, even those we have never met. In answer to the questions I just posed, I think it would be hard to perceive ourselves in relation to the world in the same way we had before.

The wonderful irony of going deep within ourselves with God as our companion is that we become more attentive to the world outside us. It is a natural outgrowth of meditation; because as we draw closer to God for our own good, God draws us out for the world's good. The discipline I am talking about here is the act of *paying attention.* Through this attentiveness, we become more attuned to everyone and everything. In turn, cultivating this attentiveness to the larger world deepens and enhances our meditation. *Cosmic awareness* is a readiness to experience *awe.* It is feeling intimate with the world — macroscopically and microscopically — seeing it all as a reflection of the Creator's love. It means becoming aware of the goodness of God's creation and humankind's betrayal of it. It draws us out of our small existence into greater love and appreciation for the diversity of the world. It helps us put into perspective our place in the universe.

*Sun Flight. Ocean Flight. Mother Earth. The Falling Leaf. The Tree. The Snake Woman.* One lesson to be learned from all of them is my place in the universe. Rather than making me feel small and insignificant -- though there are times when I need to be *put in my place!* -- they create a kind of intimacy with the cosmos. I became aware that all of creation– including me – is made of the same stuff. And, in fact, we are. That makes me pay closer attention to these encounters, seeking to understand them at a deeper, more systemic level. Perhaps that explains the fascination we have with sunrises and sunsets. I also marvel at our ability to enter vast expanses of interstellar space at mind boggling speed to establish space stations that reflect sound and light waves, so that we can see what is going on thousands of miles from home instantly in our living rooms. I am fascinated with the ability in medicine to isolate the DNA molecules and determine what disease or characteristic a person will have, or to recreate a nerve or organ – or a totally new being. Cosmic Awareness is a discipline of humility. It helps create the recognition that we are a very small part of a much larger whole. This humility is important whenever we are tempted to think we have more power than we really have.

When I am digging in my garden, placing tiny seeds hopefully into the earth, I cannot forget the embrace of Mother Earth or the feeling of *becoming* tree. That presses me to care greatly and gently for this earth -- the way it is used and abused. I am reminded that it was only given for our care, not for our own selfish purposes.

*Snake Woman* was a graphic reminder of my connection with women all over the world who struggle with the same things I do -- women who have much less freedom and a fraction of the resources that I have. I recall my first spiritual director, who lay dying from cancer and in great pain. I strained to think of something I could say or do that would relieve his agony. He admonished me to quit trying. His awareness had moved beyond his own body and its pain. He imagined that his pain was also felt by many others around the world, and if he could take some of it on for them, knowing he would die soon, he wished to do so. He truly had found his place in the universe.

Once we catch a glimpse into the larger sphere of life and become aware of our link to all that is, we experience the world differently. It is not simply that we love sunsets more or start recycling or contribute to humanitarian concerns in Zimbabwe. We also become more aware of dynamic forces which hold more sway in people's lives than individual decision-making, personal freedom, or the power of positive thinking. We are an integral part of a grand web of connections.

A family for instance has its own emotional field which connects its members and influences strongly how they act. This family might behave in ways that would be totally foreign to another family and, perhaps foreign to one member outside the family system. Individuals who belong to gangs or cults do things with the group that they would never do on their own. If this is true of small groups, it is also true of the universe. If we do not pay attention to the web we are in we could get stuck, losing our identity or even our life.

How do we get unstuck? All of the disciplines help, but I have also found that there is a powerful influence through our imaginations and through story. At one point in my life I had a passion for reading books about wizards, dragons and time travel. C.S. Lewis' *Space Trilogy or The Lion, the Witch and the Wardrobe* series, Madeleine L'Engle's *Wrinkle in Time*, Ursula LeGuin's *Earthsea Trilogy*. I read Ann McCaffrey, Raymond Feist, Marion Zimmer Bradley and many others who captured my imagination and set it free. I read them all as if my life depended on it. Maybe it did! But I got to worrying about their subject matter not being in line with my Christian faith journey. When I explored this question with my spiritual director, he suggested that perhaps these stories satisfied the mystical craving I had which was not being met in my religious life at the time. That made perfect sense to me, because I missed the experience of receiving bread and wine each week, symbols of Christ, which *transported* me out of real time into sacred time.

I realize now, however, that there was even more to it. In all these books, the disabled, the underdog, the woman, the child or the exiled man is called upon to do extraordinary things to save his people. The destiny of the world rests on their willingness to acknowledge their gift and call. The great cosmic struggle of good and evil is personified in amazing characters, some of whom die and others break through countless barriers and triumph. Their resiliency and fortitude are clearly beyond the capabilities of a normal person — yet I was drawn into the possibility of accomplishing the impossible like they had. While at times the hero's hope would fade, always it was restored in the end and was transformed in the process.

This might sound like a huge distraction from the traditional spiritual path, but I think it may resemble a variation on steps in the dance of the spirit. It might even look like a sharp divergence from the Scripture which provides my spiritual framework — but I don't think so. Jesus called together the "lost and the least," had many adventures with countless barriers, died and triumphed in the end. He brought together a motley bunch of men and women to share a meal of bread and wine which transformed the world. Almost 2,000 years later we are still eating the bread and drinking the wine that represent God's cosmic love and victory over evil. As we eat this meal, we are transported through time to the very table where it was first served. Then we are empowered to become better people, to triumph over difficulties, to be of good heart and courage and to love more. Are these stories so very different?

Stories offer us images to expand our understanding of the world. They raise up possibilities for the marginalized or least honored in society to win or to break out of invisible chains. They also offer wonderful flights of imagination. To my mind, a major ingredient in prayer is imagination. Imagining gives us a way to believe that all will be well and the courage to live into that future. Imagining that one can endure or succeed or rise above a challenge. Imagining offers a way out of the narrow confines we generally place on ourselves. Imagining allows us to empathize more fully with one another or see new possibilities for solving a difficult problem. Imagination triggers creativity which makes the world more beautiful, more sensitive, more open. Within the framework of faith, it offers hope and points toward a God who is both grounded in human life and larger than the vast expanse of interstellar space.

Cosmic Awareness is a discipline of humility. It helps create the recognition that we are a very small part of a much larger whole; and, given our nature of trying to control more than we can, to exert more power than we should, or to see our reflection larger than is true, this is a very good thing.

# An Attitude of Compassion
## (Or, Acting in Concert with God)

It is in the effects and deeds following afterward that one discerns the value of prayer… If we fail to love our neighbor, we are lost.

Teresa of Avila

I recall visiting a friend who lived in Washington, D.C. Naturally, we planned to do our bit of sight-seeing, walking from gallery to gallery and monument to monument. I always enjoy seeing the city; but I am also unnerved by the sight of so many people living on the streets. Walking with my friend was different, however. Most people study the sidewalk in front of their feet, are suddenly engaged in conversation or just look the other way when they pass the scruffy men and women who hold out their cups for money. My friend was different. He always reached into his pocket, took out some change, put it in the cup and gave the man a smile. Sometimes it was just a quarter. We rarely missed a step or a word in our conversation. It was clear that this pattern of generosity was a natural part of his life.

We never talked about this out-of-the-ordinary habit. What could I say? Why did you do that? Don't you know they will just spend it on alcohol or drugs? Or they could get a job if they really wanted to! Or what good will a quarter do anyway? To tell him what a fine, generous man he was did not seem appropriate to his ingenuous act. But the image of his encounters remains with me. I finally came to see it not so much as an act of generosity, but as an act of *compassion*. A quarter was not going to make or break that street person's life, but the smile, the simple response of my friend, went to and beyond that person's well-being. In that moment, the habits of cynicism and hard-heartedness were interrupted by an Attitude of Compassion, moving past charity into relationship.

Compassion is when the inner life and the outer life meet in natural acts of goodness, caring, generosity and justice. Compassion emerges quite freely from a life of interior prayer. Prayer allows our instincts to care about the people and creation around us to flow through us and move into action. In return, a life rooted in prayer grounds compassionate acts in love and makes them life-giving and truthful. They become energizing, not burdensome. They unite us with the loving intentions of God, which only we can enact by way of our humanity. We humans must act for and with other humans on behalf of God -- for and with creation on behalf of God.

I believe the Attitude of Compassion, or *Acting in Concert with God,* may be described as a process: observing and being attentive to the needs around us; discerning our role in addressing the needs; and, moving discernment into action. That is not to say that doing good deeds always takes this neat course. Sometimes we perform compassionate acts without premeditation. After all, it is in our essential nature to be compassionate. We are moved by the pain of another human being because we know it could just as easily be our pain. An Attitude of Compassion moves us out of self-centeredness to other-centeredness. When we are engaged in the discipline of prayer and have put down the roots which ground us deeply in God's love, we can, with strength, reach out into the world to touch others.

Observing and being attentive to the needs around us take a shift of focus. I vividly recall the moment I entered the small room at the Phillips Gallery in Washington, D.C. to experience Renoir's *The Boating Party*. This painting takes up the better part of one wall. The other three walls contained paintings of other impressionists, but this painting was featured alone. I had been admiring and appreciating the art in the other rooms, but when I saw this particular painting, my focus shifted immediately. It was as if a whole new dimension opened up, and I was drawn into it. I sat on the bench directly in front of the picture and could almost hear the people of the *Party* talking and laughing. The light sparkled off the wine glasses as if the sun were really shining at that moment. I even wondered if the little dog would begin barking. In short, I became much more attentive to this painting, while others passed around me much as I had done earlier with the other paintings. Sometimes we pass through life glancing at what is happening around us as if we are asleep, convinced at some deep level that there is nothing new that can touch us. Then something or some person steps into our field of vision quite unexpectedly, and our focus shifts. We are drawn in to see details, feel emotions, observe interactions, with new understanding, which then opens up a new space within us.

Cultivating this attentiveness is part of the spiritual journey, the mystical way. This is where it becomes a discipline. It is not forced or artificial. It means intentionally placing ourselves in situations which may open us to new life. One experience of open attentiveness leads to another. We develop the ability to experience life more fully around us. It may be pure beauty, as in the painting, or it may be the loneliness and despair in the street person

In another big city experience, I walked the streets of Manhatten with a seasoned social worker and a small group of clergy. She was associated with the John Huess House, which provides meals and support for the homeless in their neighborhood – Wall Street. I remembered my friend in Washington as I observed this young woman approach the people on the benches and sidewalks, asking about their lives, if they had eaten, inviting them to come to the Huess House. As with the Renoir painting, I was moved past the quick glance and quick judgment of ragged clothes and matted hair to see them in their desperation and fear. These were people with stories and broken lives behind their street masks. As we returned to the House, one person in our group wept openly, for he, too, had experienced this attentive observation which opens our hearts to compassion. It is as Henri Nouwen described in his book, *Reaching Out*, during a conversation with a former student. The young man and he had shared a good deal of meaningful silence. Then the student remarked, "When I look at you, it is as if I am in the presence of Christ." Nouwen's response moved the conversation even deeper, "It is the Christ in you that recognizes the Christ in me."[33]

In the moments of true attentiveness to another person or even creation, we may experience the Holy in a unifying way. Our very souls are connected to Christ when our hearts have been opened enough to see the Christ in another.

Observation alone, even attentive observation, is not enough. Once our hearts have been opened, we are invited to walk in, look around and see what we can do to respond. This is a great act of courage, for *discernment* means honestly -- really honestly -- considering ourselves and how we might act in concert with God. To what actions are we being called? What would fit our nature? What would stretch us into new realms of experience? What might press us to lower internal walls of cynicism, anger, apathy, self-doubt, or fear, which we so carefully have constructed to protect our broken hearts? Discernment is the process of seeking an honest, open heart, so that what we decide to do with our lives is a reflection of that honesty. The work of discernment is pulling down the walls, stone by stone, until we have a clear view of our heart's desire.

When we get that clear view we can begin to *take action*. Compassion is more than a good feeling or an emotional response. The God of Compassion invites us to become involved in the loving of and caring for the world, and that requires us to *do* something for it. Thankfully, not everyone is asked to do the same things. My mystical images are not yours. My call is not yours. The world may need what I have to offer, but it also needs what you can offer. Of all three steps in this process of compassion, this third requires the most courage, for it means living our faith openly and publicly after we have identified what it is we are to do.

It took me eight years finally to acknowledge that my job in the world is to be a priest. I fought with the call, struggled with the pros and cons, denied it, built a pretty good case against it, and, at last, I recognized it as the most honest response to my heart's desire. It became utterly irresistible. I could no longer deny God's call. Then the more I pursued the call, the more I realized how much I was doing *with passion*. My heart was engaged to the extent that my own fears and self-concerns were gently replaced with deep caring for the people I was called to serve. The original objections and resistance had to do with me. The end result had to do with others.

The process of an Attitude of Compassion does not just mean the big decisions in life – like deciding what our true vocation might be. It is also the small things, like giving quarters recklessly to any street person who passes. It may mean contributing financially to an organization that supports your deep concerns; or it may mean getting involved in serving the people of your concern. It may be that you are called to make food baskets for the hungry or to walk the streets inviting people to come in for shelter. You may be called to fight actively and vigorously for the rights of any group of people, or it may be that you are called to pay special attention to your attitudes toward that group in your daily life.

The truth is that we can do any number of good works without any conscious discernment. The risk in that is that it will not be sustainable in the long run, because the roots of prayer have not been planted deeply enough. Our motivation may not be very honorable. Impulsive actions often are short term. Passionate actions contain sustainable energy. One meal may quiet a growling hunger, but it will take more than one meal to awaken hope and satisfy deeper needs. Without compassion – heart, mind and body working together – we may be robbed of the God-centered strength we need to continue.

I realize I have used the word *compassion* much more broadly than it is usually used. But I think the word itself represents the life and energy that is required to describe the working of the heart. All the disciplines I have described lead us to this point – acting with heart – sharing the passion. They give us resting places and time to consider, but eventually, we must recognize our call to live out God's love in the world, acting in concert with God. Such actions are the places where Mystery enters, turning ordinary experiences into the extraordinary.

*Living from the Center* is the acknowledgment that we cannot live our spiritual lives separate from our embodied, everyday lives. What we believe, how we experience God, what we value as priorities, all contribute to how we interact with others and the world around us. In fact, the clear message from scripture and the saints is a mandate to nurture our spiritual lives – our relationship with God – in order to live better in the world. To live *from the Center* means precisely to act out in love what we discover to be true in our hearts. Whether we seek something called spirituality, holiness, mystical experiences or simply an awareness of the presence of God, the route to it is through our humanness, complete with our strengths and our weaknesses, our joy and our pain, our triumphs and our shortcomings.

*Living from the Center* builds upon the other disciplines and draws us toward God in a very personal way. It may also draw us back to the other disciplines to strength our foundation. The disciplines in this section send us back out into the world, strengthened by God's love, to put our actions where our hearts are. The discipline of *commitment* recognizes our need to be with another person or persons. It challenges our willingness to risk intimacy, allowing ourselves to be totally honest and vulnerable. It encourages the release of previous pain, anger or fear in order to learn new ways of trusting. When we stay long enough, risk enough, and trust anew, we discover we are changed.

*Cosmic Awareness* gives us a sense of our place in the world, not just as we move within our comfortable circle of family and friends, or familiar culture, but beyond. Without an appreciation of God's greater creation, we set ourselves up to be insulated, narrow and lacking vision. We miss the fullness of God, and we may become blind to the needs in the world which we could serve. *Cosmic Awareness* give us perspective and includes us more fully in promoting the goodness of creation and repairing or preventing the destruction of creation.

*Compassion*, as a discipline, demands more from us. It is not merely feeling sorry for another person. It means that we must pay particular attention to the needs and injustices around us. It requires that we discern the call of our hearts to serve others in need or to help correct injustice. Then we must move into action, whether it is in small ways or greater involvement. *Compassion* is acting in concert with God and because of God's love.

# Conclusion

Picture, if you can, a large block of wonderfully veined marble with Michelangelo standing beside it, chisel and hammer in hand. He walks around it, touches it, closes his eyes to "see" what might be in that block. He imagines how he can carefully shape a beautiful figure out of a solid block. Then, he begins to remove all the stone that is not the statue. He does not add anything, but he removes what is no longer needed so the figure can be seen clearly. The art of revealing beauty lies in removing what conceals it. This, too, is the work of the spiritual disciplines.

God has already created the beauty that is each one of us, but over time, we have become hidden by expectations of others, fears, broken relationships, deep grief, jealousy, anger – any of the very human experiences that amount to our living. All these emotions and events may pile up around us and block from our own sight the real beauty of our original creation. For some of us it may take a number of methods to chip away at the excess, unneeded protection we have built up. For all of us it takes the help of others to see our potential. The spiritual disciplines are tools in the art of inner sculpting. They engage our self-scrutiny, but they also allow light to shine on our work from many angles. They invite God – in any of God's many forms and names – into the project which gives us dimension. They involve us with the world – immediately and in the most cosmic way – which gives us perspective.

The mystical way is, quite simply, coming to know ourselves better and God more intimately. This path is available to anyone, though there have been some who are drawn more completely into it. We can know God in our ordinary living. We can be aware of God in the most mundane situations. We can seek God in the most common places. We must look for the mystical moments in our lives as they appear to us, not as they appear to another person. This diversity is the beauty of Creation.

The disciplines keep us focused. They are tools that can knock off huge chunks of unneeded protection, and they can carve gently and carefully at the vulnerable details. The disciplines, these spiritual tools, are acts of love which bring us closer to ourselves and closer to God. Unlike the marble, however, we do not remain immobile and beautiful only from the outside. We become more approachable, more able to give and to receive in our relationships, better able to appreciate and serve the world around us. Our relationships are enriched. We are not just changed, we are transformed. This is the beauty of the mystical way. For this, we may give thanks.

# Blessings

There is a large body of water —
       perhaps a lake — perhaps a sea.
            This water lies very still — no wind —
                 not  a breeze — even the clouds pause.
It is as if the WHOLE earth
       is holding its breath.
We do not know what is happening below the surface . . .
       but, above
            it remains absolutely calm —
                a mirror-like surface,
                    silvery, shimmering blue.
THEN,
       without warning the water is broken! —
            from nowhere a pebble is dropped
                on this watery veneer.
       An EXCLAMATION of water
            LEAPS into the air.
If you could observe in slow motion,
       you would see a small tower emerge
            with water walls
                topped off with sparkling spires.
       Then, the little pieces of the tower break off . . .
            and make multiple explosions
                in the unsuspecting surface.
       As the tower collapses,
            returning to its place of conception,
                reverberations pulse out
                   from the point of impact…
                      ripple… after ripple spread out
           in an ever widening circle of movement
                straining to reach as far as possible.
How could such a small stone
       make such a large impression?
Blessings are like that.

*An exclamation of water leaps into the air…*
        *A small tower emerges with water walls… How could such a small stone*
*make such a large impression?*

# Beatitudes

Moments of insight and understanding occur at such unexpected times. I was riding the train on my way home from a long and regular commute between Chicago and Michigan. I had an assignment to reflect on The Beatitudes (Matthew 5:1-12). These words were so familiar, I thought, what can I possibly come up with that is new? Ten of us would be preaching on the same passage. Again, what would I have to say about these statements that go against the grain of American culture and definitions of success?

I closed my eyes and asked, or more accurately, begged, for insight. I was immediately drawn into the image I have just described and then the words that follow in explanation. After the silence, I was writing furiously -- in an attempt to capture what I had seen in my head -- when the train conductor came along to collect my ticket. I was so startled, I must have jumped a foot off my seat, and my heart was beating a wild rhythm against the inside of my chest. He was apologetic and asked if I was O.K. I said I was fine -- it's nothing really.

# Beatitude Relfections

## (Or, An Attitude of Thanksgiving)

When we feel, for instance,
    in great spiritual hunger or need,
        at a time of grief or despair,
            we may experience God's BLESSING,
              much like the pebble.
At the moment of contact — the moment of knowing —
    an EXCLAMATION of love is made —
    or a gentle touch is felt —
        BLESSED ARE THE POOR IN SPIRIT.
This moment surpasses even happiness
    because we know it is a tiny glimpse
        into God's Kingdom Come.
It is the moment of unity we speak about
        every Sunday in our Eucharistic Prayers —
           when we know God's presence
              in and through us.
    At that moment we want to shout or cry
        with awe and joy and inexplicable love
We want to hold that moment of knowing God close.
    We have been BLESSED!
        Our spirits have been enriched and
           we know God in a new way.
But, it is not in the nature of a Blessing
    to be held within forever.
        Once we experience the moment when our life
        and God's Grace connect,
           the Exclamation of Blessing
              begs to be released.
The ripples begin to flow out from us.
Sometimes, we are conscious of the outflowing.
    We may tell others
        about our encounter with God, or
           we may be moved to seek others
    who also experience a poor spirit,
        and we try to tell them they, too, are BLESSED.

Sometimes, the ripples flow out from us
       and we are not aware.
I met a young woman on the street one day.
       She had had car trouble
          and needed a quarter to call a wrecker.
            She asked me for the quarter.
     I said — Sure — and gave her one.
Not far from us was an old woman,
       dressed shabbily, carrying a large shopping bag.
        She had listened and watched
          the quarter exchange.
As I left the young woman,
       I walked toward the old woman —
         She hurried a little to meet me…
           came right up to me… grinned…
        and said, *Could I have one of those, too?*
     I said, *Sure* — and gave her the quarter.
Who was blessing whom?
That old woman probably never knew
      how her BLESSEDNESS rippled out to meet me.
        BLESSED ARE THE PURE IN HEART!
Then there are those
      who show a gentle spirit.
        They are the ones who are loving
          and most vulnerable —
to them, God promises the WHOLE EARTH.
        It is a good thing, too.
         They are the ones who care deeply for
RAIN FOREST TREES . . . and OIL-SOAKED BIRDS…
        for WOUNDED AND BROKEN PEOPLE.
They are blessed, indeed.
Yet, this world of water… and BLESSINGS…
      is a large one,
        and the ripples move farther and farther away
          from the moment of Blessed explosion.
In truth,
      pebbles are being dropped all over…
        and ripples are meeting ripples.
      MERCY is shown and
        MERCY is returned.

It IS sad, though, that so many pebbles drop
            and go totally unnoticed.
                    It is the same with BLESSINGS.
Perhaps, there would be more PEACEMAKERS,
            more CHILDREN OF GOD,
                    if more Blessings were noticed.
Perhaps there would be
            more workers for justice and equality.
                    These blessings require action, intent.
But, even so, God does not *demand* response or Thanks.
            God just keeps on blessing us —
                    generation after generation,
                            around the globe, across time —
                                    and right into God's eternal Kingdom.
And the ripples gather on the beach
            marking the shoreline, always making it new.
BLESSINGS do this.
            Blessings touch us within.
                    Blessings touch others through us.
                            Blessings are a promise for our future.
How could such a small stone
            make such a large impression?
                    That is the amazing part of blessings --
                            Yet, they are missed every day.
The important thing is -- NOT to miss yours.

# Comments and Acknowledgements

Mystical truth is the unsummoned presence of the beyond. I believe it is the deepest level of truth available to human experience. It means that the opposite of a grasped truth is a truth that does the grasping. The initiative in seeking and finding such truth is generally not one's own but comes unbidden by human resolve or expectation. Every level of truth above this can be experienced, comprehended, and articulated, whereas mystical truth is confined almost entirely to the category of experience. The mystical, while common in human experience, cannot be fully comprehended or satisfactorily articulated. It is the sensation of being taken hold of in one's depth by an exalting power that lifts one's spirit above the ordinary.

Bennett J. Sims[34]

You have ventured with me into the area of mystical spirituality in a very personal way. I have shared with you my experiences of God, and I have invited you to reflect on your experiences. This is risky for both of us, for we are not all that comfortable with making our private lives public. Yet, it is an exciting thing to know someone else has been touched by God as we have. It is reassuring to realize the experience we have been hiding for so long – thinking that it was a little touch of crazy, or simply unexplainable – was a gift, a moment with God, and perfectly acceptable in the realm of prayer and spirituality. Other ordinary people have experienced God in a direct and memorable way.

The experiences that I have shared were shaped by my personality, my life history, my faith and my world view. All of them came to me *before* I was ordained, so ordination is by no means a guarantee or a prerequisite of mystical encounters. It seems to me that God enters our lives in ways that we can recognize because God knows us all too well. You may be a musician and experience God in the union of one instrument with another, notes dancing in the treble balancing the strength of the bass. You may be a person who loves words and finds inspiration not through images but through language, by the way it creates feelings and teases thoughts. You may be a person of a particular culture or nationality that provides ways which are totally foreign to me, yet are filled with Spirit and wisdom for you. You may be a farmer or gardener and find that the land, your animals, and the cycle of the seasons shape your life and influence your experience of God. You may have had a difficult even abusive childhood and traditional images or references to God are more hurtful than healing. Who you are and what you have experienced helps shape how you know God.

Such is the nature of Mystery which seeks in whatever way possible to meet us – if only we would extend our hands and open our hearts. Of course, it never feels that simple, for traveling along the committed way of faith is not like following a well-designed map laid out especially for our journey. To make it even more difficult, we become distracted along the way and lose our sense of direction, or worse yet we lose our sense of purpose. This is where the routine of the disciplines comes in. Perhaps, you will find a place for them as well.

Over five years ago I had a strong feeling that it was time that I share some of the encounters I have had with God so that others might be enabled to accept the encounters they have had. While this has not been an easy assignment, it has been an adventure! The process of writing this book has been enlivening, informative, and life-shaping. The more I work with these experiences the more insights and complexities I discover in them. The more I share these moments and understandings with others the more I realize people are hungry to know that God is present and intimately available to ordinary people. And, so , when my resolve lagged or blocks appeared to my writing, or I found ways to talk myself out of the project, someone always appeared to encourage me, or the original internal urging became too strong to ignore. And so, I have come to this point.

From the beginning, I had a sense that these encounters should be visual as well as expressed in writing. The only person I knew who had the talent and spiritual perception, and was connected through love to me, was my brother, Don Thomas. Our first project together was the booklet cover for my ordination. Trusting completely that he could come up with something great, I read him the scriptural passage I had chosen for the service. Within a short time, he sent a drawing which astounded me and captured in simple lines the essence of the scriptural message. From this experience I knew we could tackle this project together. As we began, it was clear that he knew what was needed, without much explanation from me. He drew out of my encounters images that wonderfully reflected my experiences, but he also painted images that stretched me to see broader implications for my previously very personal, hoarded experiences. I feel privileged to have shared this project with such a talented, soul-filled artist.

I marvel at the *coincidences* that made it possible for me to meet and study with Ron and Eleanor DelBene. Ron opened a very important door to prayer for me and introduced me to the spiritual disciplines. Eleanor, a woman of healing and insight, showed me how we are connected, body, mind and spirit, and how we must attend to them all.

128

I am also grateful to the two people who have been in on this from the beginning and encouraged me every step of the way, my husband, Jim Glennie and my dear friend, Linda MacDonald. Everyone should be so lucky! They provided support and understanding in so many ways, both affirming and challenging. I am also grateful to my class of brave parishioners who decided to find out what their priest was about in her still unpolished book about direct experiences with God. They gave me important feedback and nerve to go on. Anna Graham edited my work with skill and sensitivity. Many people I encountered along the way did not even know they were giving me encouragement for a project they didn't know I was creating.

Thank you.

# *Appendix*

## About the Illustrator

Don Thomas is a Design Principal at BWBR Architects in St. Paul, Minnesota. His previous work includes illustrations for books on creativity and personal grief. Working in the design field for 20 years, he has also taught workshops in design, drawing and creativity. Don received his BFA from the University of Wisconsin-Stout a long time ago and lives with his family in St. Paul. This is his first collaboration with his sister, Jannel who has graciously taught him the value of searching for wonder.

### *Introduction Notes*

When Jannel first approached me with the idea of illustrating her book, I'll admit my first reaction was to find a very polite way to say no. To be comfortable with the idea, I had to jump a few emotional hurdles. The largest one was questioning my confidence in the ability to honestly understand and visually translate her mystical experiences. Luckily, faith can come in small steps and Jannel was very patient.

From the first reading of her journals, I was impressed with the strength and honesty of her experiences. I'm not sure what I expected, but the vividness and intensity drew me closer to understanding why she was so passionate about this project and I was soon wrapped up in the warm support of her immediate family and dedicated associates.

More than the final product, I cherish the time spent with Jannel in our long weekend retreats at her home. We set up a makeshift studio in her dining room where I'd sketch loose ideas for each encounter. She would keep the coffee coming and beautiful music in the air. After a time, we'd discuss and compare the sketches with the journals. Usually, I had more questions than answers and we soon developed into a very collaborative team. I'd return home and finish up the renderings, anxiously awaiting her response.

I hope you enjoy the sketches as much as I enjoyed making them. Good luck and Godspeed in your search for the sacred in the ordinary.

Often, visualizing your ideas can create a deeper understanding. You do not need to be an artist to do this, however and should not put the burden of creating "real artwork" on yourself. Below are some ideas to help illustrate your thoughts, dreams and experiences.

## *"Visual Listening"*

If you are uncomfortable with drawing or painting, search for images or items to illustrate your ideas. Begin by writing either words or phrases. It is best to keep them short and simple, like *Love, Warmth, Passion, Healing Spaces, Family,* etc. Then search a wide range of sources for visual inspiration, including magazines, books, newspapers and postcards. Find images that touch you, such as an image of a sun-washed green meadow with a wildflowers and a blue sky for the word: "Warmth". Try not to analyze or edit your response, just connect words to images quickly. Once you have selected a variety of images, arrange them in a loose collage or portfolio that corresponds to your words. Look for relationships and connections.

This can also be accomplished by collecting actual objects such as toys, rocks, leaves or tools.

## *Drawing and Painting*

Select simple materials. These do not need to be expensive art supplies. Begin by drawing or painting a simple sketch of your idea. Decide from the beginning of your activity that you do not need to show anyone your drawings and you will be freer in your expression. Often, either music or natural sounds can enhance this process.

There are two general types of drawings or paintings: representational and impressionistic.

### Representational

Representational drawings illustrate something recognizable: a chair, fireplace or a person, for example. They are meant to look like the thing we are thinking about. The key to these sketches is give yourself permission to be inaccurate, to exaggerate or embellish.

Focus all your thoughts on the paper and begin by either drawing around the object, "finding" it on the paper, or start from the center and draw outward. Remember, you are trying to illustrate something very personal, so you can render it any way you like. The important thing is not the accuracy of the sketch but the process of drawing. As you draw, you will remember more about the event and understand it better as you make it real on paper.

### Impressionistic

Impressionistic drawing is from an emotional point of view, drawing what you feel rather that what you see. Center yourself and draw or paint spontaneously. You have an endless variety of ways to create your "visual language". Drawing jagged, harsh lines with caustic colors could say you are angry or swooping, gentle shapes in to illustrate hope. Draw what you feel and resist the temptation to represent something specific out of the images.

Finding ways to visually enhance your spiritual journey is an exciting process. The above examples are very brief descriptions intended to get you started. I encourage you to grab a pencil and explore the possibilities!

# Study Guide and
# Suggestions for Further Reflection

Following are some suggestions, questions, and prayerful – even playful – activities which may help you engage the material in this book more completely. The purpose would always be to provide a way for you to come to know God more intimately and yourself more clearly.

This could be done as an individual. Or a group might want to come together to share the experiences and insights. Some exercises may be done while the group gathers together, or you may decide to have individuals explore certain activities on their own and then return to the group to share feelings or ideas that emerged. Of course, you may think of other methods of exploration – feel free!

## Encounters and Reflections

Finding the right words to describe a mystical experience is almost impossible. It is similar to explaining a dream to someone. In dreams time and space are almost irrelevant. You can seem to be doing two or more very different things at once that defy rational experience. It is similar with mystical experiences – words are hard to find. We say these experiences are ineffable, difficult to grasp, illusory. But it is still good to give it a try. It is also true that in writing or telling about the experience, details may come alive that you hadn't appreciated before. You may even gain some new understanding that had been eluding you.

First, you may want to reflect on the following questions as triggers for recalling an event that is *ineffable.*

- When have you been involved in something when you were totally unaware of the time passing? Time has become irrelevant or you felt, somehow, not in present time?

- Describe a time when you were so overcome with joy or exultation and a feeling of well-being took over your whole body? Or perhaps it was a moment of unexplainable tears.

- Recall a memory of feeling totally connected to another object (say, of creation, like trees, grass, sun, moon, ocean, etc.) or another person?

- When have you sensed a knowing that surprised you and you realized you had not initiated the thought , idea or feeling? Perhaps you had an insight about a decision or a relationship.

- Now try to describe your experience in writing or to another person. Reflect on the experience of putting it into another form. What new insights did you gain? How might it have been connected to another similar incident that you had forgotten? How did you feel after telling or writing it?

- Each of the Reflections following Encounters contains some questions to stimulate further reflections. What did you discover for yourself in considering these questions?

# The Illustrations

The artist, Don Thomas, read the encounters that I had described and without much prompting on my part, drew what he saw. Sometimes I was quite surprised by what he drew. Other times I had to coach him to help him get past his initial feelings stirred by the encounter to draw something close to what I had seen. This process was very enriching to both of us. We both understood that more could be drawn or said about each one.

- Just as Don could see things in my descriptions that elicited images for him. I could see meaning in the drawings he made. Without reading my encounter what story might you tell about a particular illustration that attracts you? Also select one that presents a block or difficult feelings.

- You may want to alter one of the drawings. What changes would you make? Try drawing it yourself or make notes in the margin.

- Select an illustration and place it before you. Take 5-10 minutes and just gaze at the drawing being open to what it might say to you.

- *The Wounded Heart* is clearly a different quality drawing! The act of using color on paper to reflect an inner state of being can be very helpful in sorting out a problem or working through a sense of no feelings at all. You will need large sheets of paper (newsprint works fine), pastels or crayons, a CD or tape player and some music. If you are alone, you can select the music that best matches your mood. If you are doing this in a group, you might want to select a piece that provides a variety of moods. Create a place of silence. Lay the paper and pastels out before you and wait for the Spirit to lead you. I suggest you use your non-dominant hand. Select the colors that leap out at you – and draw whatever comes.

When you are finished think about the feelings that the process of drawing elicited. Turn the drawing around and look at it from all angles – what does it suggest to you. How do you feel after the drawing? Try not to judge what you drew. You may find it helpful to have others look at it and suggest what they see in it. You can always disagree!

# Suggestions (The Spiritual Disciplines)

There are many ways you could explore the disciplines for yourself. I have suggested a few ways to think about them, but the best way to know them is to try them.

## Being in Place

- How would you describe your relationship with God as a child? How would you describe it now? What names, descriptors or verbs best describe God for you? How does your name for God reflect your experience of God in your life?

- How do you communicate with God now? How do you define prayer? What have you been taught about prayer that is helpful – or not?

- My definition of prayer is quite broad and includes many different activities. When have you experienced these activities but never thought of them as prayer? How might you be more intentional about seeing god more fully in your life?

- Telling God what we want is the easy part of praying. How can you create a space, both time and location, to listen for God? When have you sensed God's presence in your everyday living?

- How comfortable are you with silence? Is there too little or too much in your life? If there is too little you may want to plan some time for it. If there is too much silence you may want to reflect on how you might actively seek God in it.

## Growing in Faith

- I use the image of journey several times to describe the way we grow in faith. We move from life experience to life experience and along the way we come to understand God differently. Try making a map of your faith journey. When were the times you experienced God clearly? Where were the sharp turns, mountains, valleys, swamps or meadows? What signs moved you on or slowed you up? What vehicles helped or hindered your progression?

After you draw this map share it with someone else. The telling often will reveal new insights or patterns. Be sure to describe where you are now.

- What role has study played in your life? Where do you get your new ideas? What kind of books, classes, people or groups have influenced you and your faith? Referring to the list of "things to beware" on page 78-79, which of these most challenges you?

- Who has made significant contributions toward your decision-making and faith growth? What qualities did you most appreciate in them? How might you benefit now by having a person or group participate in your spiritual journey?

- Describe your most memorable ritual experience. Describe the feelings you had during and after the experience. How many of your senses were involved? Did it involve body actions? What new or familiar connections did you feel to other people or to God? What was the story that was being told?

### *Living from the Center*

Living from the Center calls us to action or may pull us back to the beginning. We may come to know God intimately through any one of these disciplines and then be drawn to another, then back to the former in a deeper way. All of the disciplines are building blocks, or as Maria Harris has described them, as steps in the Dance of the Spirit.[35]

- What has been your experience with the intersection of the spiritual life and your life commitments? List the commitments that you are currently in – or, perhaps past commitments. Reflect on how you have experienced risk, trust and change in them.

- When did you realize enormity of the universe? Where do you go to feel connected to the earth or the water or any of Creation? How could you stay in touch with that feeling of being connected? What stories expand your world or trigger your imagination? How does God fit in?

- "Compassion is when the inner life and the outer life meet in natural acts of goodness, caring, generosity and justice." (p. ___) Take a walk in the city or a busy neighborhood, or a business park or factory. Keep your eyes open especially for any acts of compassion. Read the newspapers carefully looking for particular needs or activities that stimulate you. Listen for God's calling you to action.

You may reproduce this Appendix if it is helpful for your group. Enjoy the journey!

# Additional Sources

Beer, Fran. Women and Mystical Experience in the Middle Ages. The Boydell Press, 1992.

*The Book of Common Prayer,* New York: The Church Hymnal Corporation, 1979.

Brunn, Emilie Zum and Georgette Epiney-Burgard. Women Mystics in Medieval Europe, New York: Paragon House, 1989.

Campbell, Camille. Meditations with Teresa of Avila. Santa Fe, New Mexico: Bear & Company, Inc., 1985.

Flanagan, Sabina. Hildegard of Bingen, 1098-1179: A Visionary Life. Routledge, 1989.

Flinders, Carol Lee. At the Root of this Longing: Reconciling a Spiritual Hunger and a Feminist Thirst. HarperSanFrancisco, 1998.

Flinders, Carol Lee. Enduring Grace. HarperSanFrancisco.

Harris, Maria. Dance of the Spirit. New York: Bantam Books, 1989.

Hildegard of Bingen. Illuminations of Hildegard of Bingen, Commentary by Matthew Fox, O.P., Santa Fe, New Mexico: Bear & Company, Inc., 1985.

Holy Bible: The New Revised Standard Version. New York: Oxford University Press, 1989.

Julian of Norwich: Showings. Trans. Edmund Colledge, O.S.A. and James Walsh, S.J., The Classics of Western Spirituality Series. New York: Paulist Press, 1978.

McGinn, Bernard. The Foundations of Mysticism, Origins to the Fifth Century. New York: Crossroad, 1991.

Newman, Barbara. Sister of Wisdom: St. Hildegard's Theology of the Feminine. University of California Press, 1987.

Soul of the World: A Modern Book of Hours. Ed. Phil Cousineau, Photographs by Eric Lawton. HarperSanFrancisco, 1993.

<u>Teresa of Avila: The Interior Castle</u>, Trans. Kieran Kavanaugh, O.C.D. and Otilio Rodriguez, O.C.D. The Classics of Western Spirituality Series. New York: Paulist Press, 1979.

Underhill, Evelyn. <u>The Spiritual Life</u>. Wilton, Conn: Morehouse Barlow, 1955.

# Notes

1. This prayer is an ancient form of prayer which has been taught in many different ways. Most recently it has been described as the "Breath Prayer." Ron DelBene, with Mary and Herb Montgomery, <u>The Breath of Life</u>, (Nashville: Upper Room Books, 2<sup>nd</sup> Print 1995).

2., Evelyn Underhill, <u>Mysticism</u> (New York: Image Books, Doubleday, 1990, (lst published 1911) 24.

3. Kenneth Leach, <u>Experiencing God: Theology as Spirituality</u>, 332.

4. Marsha Sinetar, <u>Ordinary People as Monks and Mystics</u>, (Mahwah, NJ: Paulist Press, 1986).

5. Underhill, <u>Mysticism</u>, 24.

6. Henri Nouwen, <u>The Way of the Heart</u>, (New York: The Seabury Press, 1980) 20-22.

7. William Wordsworth, "Tintern Abbey," <u>Lyrical Ballads with a Few Other Poems</u>, (Bristol: Printed by Biggs and Cottle, for T.N. Longman, Paternoster-Row, London, 1798).

8. Leach, <u>Experiencing God</u>.

9. William McNamara, <u>Earthy Mysticism</u>, (currently out of print) 4.

10. "The literature of mysticism is shot through with images of enclosure. Of walled gardens, interior castles, cocoons, and beehives. There is no great mystery here. Meditation is synonymous with turning inward, and it requires that we withdraw attention from everything around us. It is all but impossible to do this if we have reason to feel self-conscious or vulnerable or apprehensive… The enclosure of women is a custom feminists have had no choice but to challenge." Carol Flinders, <u>At the Root of this Longing: Reconciling a Spiritual Hunger and a Feminist Thirst</u>, (HarperSanFrancisco, 1998) 80-82.

11. Robert Frost, "The Road Not Taken," <u>Modern American Poetry</u>, Ed. Untermeyer, Louis, 1919. <http://www.bartleby.com/104/67.html>

12. Leach, <u>Experiencing God</u>, 220.

13. Nouwen, <u>The Way of the Heart</u>, 81.

14. Jesus Prayer: *Lord Jesus Christ, Son of God, have mercy on me, a sinner.* There may be variations on the phrasing of this short invocation which originated in the Eastern Christian tradition and is meant to lead one to a stillness of heart.  It is an ancient form of prayer and was made familiar through The Way of the Pilgrim, written by an anonymous Russian layman in the middle of the nineteenth century.  Christian Spirituality: Origins to the Twelfth Century, Ed. Bernard McGinn, John Meyendorff, and Jean Leclercq, (New York: Crossroad, 1993) 403.

15. Ibid.,  412.

16. Dwight H. Judy,  Embracing God: Praying with Teresa of Avila,, (Nashville, Abingdon Press, 1996) (taken from The Way of Perfection), 44.

17. Teresa of Avila: The Interior Castle, Trans. Kieran Kavanaugh, O.C.D. and Otilio Rodriguez, O.C.D., The Classics of Western Spirituality Series, (New York: Paulist Press, 1979) 39.

18. Marchiene Vroon Rienstra, Swallow's Nest: A Feminine Reading of the Psalms, (Grand Rapids, Michigan: Wm. B. Eerdmans Publishing Co., 1992) 231.

19. John Moffitt (1908-1987), "To look at any thing" from America <http://logannature.org/newsflash/newsletter/spring99/page6.html>

20. John Macquarrie, Prayer and Theological Reflection:The Study of Spirituality, Ed. Jones, Wainwright, Yarold, (New York: Oxford University Press, 1986) 585.

21. Richard J. Foster, Celebration of Discipline: The Path to Spiritual Growth, Rev. Ed.,, (HarperSanFrancisco, 1988) 186.

22. Tilden Edwards, Spiritual Friend: Reclaiming the Gift of Spiritual Direction, (New York: Paulist Press, 1980).  Edwards gives some especially helpful suggestions about finding and being spiritual friends, seeking a spiritual director and using a group as spiritual guides.

23. This particular illustration was very difficult for my brother to draw, because it clearly reminded him of a grave.  After many attempts at describing how it felt for me, I said, "It is like Mother Earth just holding me."  When I came back to see his drawing, he had used his hands as a model, and then was able to express in color and drawing what I had felt.  Also, when my oldest daughter looked at it, she commented that it looked

a lot like a birth canal! Perhaps, that is just what was happening at the time I first experienced it.

24. The Quakers or Society of Friends call a similar process a *clearness committee.* There are very specific guidelines for such a group, some of which I adapted to meet my situation at the time.

25. Teresa of Avila: <u>The Interior Castle</u>, 39.

26. Leonel L. Mitchell, <u>The Meaning of Ritual</u>, (Wilton, Conn Morehouse-Barlow, 1977) 13.

27. Elizabeth Barrett Browing, "Earth is crammed with heaven," <u>Aurora Leigh and Other Poems</u>, Ed. John Robert Glorney Bolton, Julia Bolton Holloway, (Harmondsworth: Penguin, 1995).

28. All quotes offered on this page are taken from: <u>Songs of the Earth: A Tribute to Nature in Word and Image</u> (Philadelphia, PA: Running Press Book Publishers, 1995 (Printed in China).

29. Margaret Farley, <u>Personal Commitments, Making, Keeping, Breaking</u> (San Francisco: Harper & Row, Publishers, 1986) 10, 18.

30. Michael Downey, "Making a Way," <u>Weavings, A Journal of the Christian Spiritual Life</u>, (The Upper Room; Volume IX, Number 4, July/August 1994) 8-9.

31. Evelyn Underhill, <u>The Spiritual Life: Great Spiritual Truths for Everyday Life</u> (Oxford: Oneworld Publications, Ltd., 1993) 16-19, 27.

32. From "Eucharistic Prayer C", <u>The Book of Common Prayer</u>, (The Church Hymnal Corporation, 1979) 370.

33. Henri J. M. Nouwen, <u>Reaching Out: The Three Movements of the Spiritual Life</u>, (Garden City NY: Doubleday & Company, Inc., 1975) 31.

34. Bennett Sims, <u>Servanthood: Leadership for the Third Millennium</u>, (Boston: Cowley Publications, 1997) 64.

35. Maria Harris, <u>Dance of the Spirit</u>. (New York: Bantam Books, 1989).

# Thoughts

# Thoughts

# Thoughts

# Thoughts

# Thoughts

# Order Additional Copies of this Book!

You can order three different ways:

1. Call (800) 932-5420

2. Visit www.greenleafbookgroup.com

3. Complete the form below and send it to:

**Greenleaf Book Group LLC**
**660 Elmwood Point, Aurora, OH 44202**

------------------------------------------------------------------------

Name _____

Address _____

City _____ State _____ Zip _____

Phone _____ Fax _____

Email _____

Each book is $20.00 with FREE shipping

Please Circle Method of Payment

Check    Visa    MasterCard    Discover    American Express

CC Number _____

Exp Date _____  Signature _____

# Order Additional Copies of this Book!

You can order three different ways:

1. Call (800) 932-5420

2. Visit www.greenleafbookgroup.com

3. Complete the form below and send it to:

**Greenleaf Book Group LLC**
**660 Elmwood Point, Aurora, OH 44202**

-------------------------------------------------------------------------

Name _____

Address _____

City _____ State _____ Zip _____

Phone _____ Fax _____

Email _____

Each book is $20.00 with FREE shipping

Please Circle Method of Payment

Check   Visa   MasterCard   Discover   American Express

CC Number _____

Exp Date _____ Signature _____